Engineering a Father

A Journey of Surviving the NICU

Ross J. Smith

Engineering A Father —A Journey of Surviving the NICU

Smith, Ross J.

Published by:

Flat Water Publishing, LLC – May 2024
Grand Haven, MI 49417
USA

ISBN 979-889412-667-8:

For Eden, Roman, and Addy

Table of Contents

Disclaimer

I am an engineer. There, now it's out in the open, but you would have figured it out on your own eventually. For starters, my wardrobe — a short-sleeve collared shirt, tucked into my khaki pants — it's a dead giveaway. Even beyond my fashion sense, there are many other technical predispositions. I use long sentences, needlessly large words, and I always implement Oxford commas when I write. I can visualize and discuss abstract scientific concepts, and then sketch them in three dimensions on my favorite graph paper. I actually understand physics, I use it in my daily job, and I explain it, loudly, to strangers. I systematically think through endless steps of complex and simple life processes. Oh, and I'm fairly certain I can solve most of the world's problems with an elaborate spreadsheet I've been developing.

I bring this all up not because it defines me and not even as an excuse for how I am. But my being an engineer is important context; a special lens refracting my perspective of the world. It helps me distinguish chaos from order; others' (often ridiculous) opinions from substantiated facts; and the painfully wrong from the obviously right. If you're wired like me, you get it. You see things the way I do. This book is for you.

As for the rest of you, don't feel left out. Even if you're not so technically intuitive, I'll bet you know someone who is. That neighbor whose garbage cans are always straight, or your uncle who still assembles and displays complicated Lego sets. You know us, you are related to one of us, or God-forbid, you might have even married one of us. There, there, we understand it's been a struggle. This book is for you too. I present it as an opportunity. Finally, you can glimpse the world through the filter of the engineering mind - the one that usually frustrates you with its quirkiness. It might be a little scary, but it might help you understand us more. And maybe we'll change a little too, actually emote once in a while, and be a little more of what you would call "normal." But probably not. Instead, we'll log another data point of your illogical behavior on the chart we're keeping in the garage while secretly hoping you'll finally see how we were right about everything all along. I mean come on, we're engineers.

Engineering a Father

Introduction

For years I wrestled with the idea of putting pen to paper, or more literally, fingers to keyboard, to actually do it, to start writing a book. Every time I considered starting, my conscience and pride ganged up on me, planting seeds of doubt.

Why would anyone want to read my *book?*

When I finally spoke the words out loud to my wife — "I'm going to write a book" — I think she wondered the same thing. Actually, I think she might still think that, and frankly, she might be right. It didn't make sense, it wasn't an efficient use of time, and there are 2.3 million new self-published books every year (I checked). The data didn't support the initiative.

My reasoning and insecurities plus my perception of her doubts plagued me, and I hung it up, multiple times. The cycle continued until one day I was talking to my friend Chris, and he unequivocally affirmed my idea and insisted that I should just do it. Just start writing. Don't plan it or overanalyze it, just write. Not analyzing is never really an option for me, but his advice struck a chord, and I realized it doesn't really matter if anyone reads it. I just need to put down on paper what's been clanking around in my head for decades.

The next struggle began as I questioned how to pull it all together, and how to express what I really wanted to say. Given my predispositions, I systematically concluded my book should be highly technical. That hypothesis spiraled around in my mind unresolved for a while until I abandoned the equations and bullet points and decided I should just tell the story.

If you know me at all, you know storytelling suits me well as I can be a bit of a talker. My dad and brother are the same way. We may not grasp it in the moment, but we like to regale others with our experiences. We are regalers. *Is that even a word?* Let's just say that it is. Once our stories get going, plan on exhaustively detailed context, stirred with (what we think are) interesting sidebars and tangents, and often a sprinkling of humor or plain, good old-fashioned indignation. The conflicts, the surprises, the absurdities, the audacity, the stupidity. We share enough excruciating minutiae that when the saga ends, you're smiling with us, or your blood is boiling with ours, just enough that we've won you over to our point of view. That, or you're just glad it's over.

Considering this particular story, I always thought it would be solely about our unexpected journey as parents to the NICU. But, while that remains the centerpiece, as I kept writing, I noticed the larger story arc connects to and is affected by many more aspects of my life; honestly, my entire life. I can already guess what you're thinking: "Entire life" sounds like an awful lot of ground to cover. You're right, it is. Perhaps worse, I'll admit I just turned forty-five (as of 2023), so if you're computing the math at home, you may be hypothesizing that I am simply having a midlife crisis. There, I said it for you, the middle-aged engineer has reached a critical point, the big parenting project is almost finished, and he's not sure what to do himself. So *that* explains this whole book writing nonsense.

I'll tell you this much, my son is absolutely convinced that this is the case. He likes to point out that I started writing a book (perhaps the most absurd thing he's ever heard) and started playing pickleball (don't knock it until you've tried it) in the span of six months. Ergo, classic midlife crisis.

Statistically, I suppose I am at about midlife, maybe even past it, but though my son makes several good points, I don't think I'm in a crisis. Not a major one anyway. I'm not looking for a sports car, or dying my slowly graying hair, or making any other uncharacteristic or unsavory life decisions. I mean, if someone wants to give me a sports car, say a new Corvette or a DeLorean, I'll certainly take it. But that's not my midlife focus. It's just time. Time to schedule a colonoscopy, but also time to write.

About You

Most of this book is about me, but let's first talk about you. You're here for some reason. What is it? Maybe you don't know that answer yet, maybe someone just suggested you read this book. If you're here for the story — I hope it is interesting, compelling, and relatable.

Perhaps you're on the threshold of parenthood and a book about becoming a father is intriguing and suddenly very relevant. Congratulations, you're about to embark on the most difficult, but most rewarding phase of your life.

Or maybe you're ending an era of parenting, and this memoir might reveal some treasured touchstones from your own experiences. Well done, you've made it, I hope your journey was rich beyond measure.

Finally, you might be here because your child is in, was recently in, or may soon be in neonatal intensive care. If this is you, I'm sorry you have to endure this chapter of life. I understand how you're feeling. The despair, the confusion, the suspension of all that you hoped and dreamed for you, and for your child. I get it. I have been there. I'm also sorry to say I can't fix the situation for you, and I can't necessarily make it hurt any less. What I can tell you is you're not alone.

Whatever your own status may be, I've traveled the road before you, at least parts of it, and through this book, you can travel some of my road with me. My hope is that reading it will help you to know my struggles, my frustrations, my fears, and my many failures. To know someone else has felt helpless, and fragile, and angry.

I also want to assure you there will be joy. Pure, unadulterated joy that fills you to the brim, and beyond. It may come in glimpses and fragments, but they will be there — be careful not to miss them.

You can get through this. You are not alone. There is a solution to this unbalanced equation. Let me tell you about it.

Part I - Before

Interrupted

I started cutting grass with a lawn mower in second grade, when I was maybe eight years old. It feels a little odd to add the phrase "with a lawnmower," but it's an important distinction.

For a year or two prior, my dad assigned me the job to trim around the trees and telephone poles with the hand clippers. Think of a big pair of scissors, only a little more robust, and spring-loaded. I could just barely squeeze the split handles together if I used both hands. It was a medieval-era device, seemingly terribly dangerous to a six-year-old, and the dark orange residue on the inner edges of the shears most assumed to be corrosion was almost certainly dried blood from a long lineage of other young boys who shouldn't have been using that tool. Not to worry though, I had been warned about the danger of cutting off my fingers, and I was scared to death of doing that very thing, so all necessary precautions had been taken.

So, yes, I was cutting grass, and it was without a mower. Not much grass, mind you, just the rogue inaccessible blades that had grown up against the various yard obstructions, but it was my job, and I did it.

In second grade I got called up to the big leagues and was assigned to cut the front yard *with the mower*. Not the whole yard, and not the expansive back yard, just the front. Still, it was a major promotion. We lived across the street from my school, and I can remember mowing during the big kids' junior high softball games, just knowing all the older students and their parents saw me and were super impressed with my hard work and lawn mowing prowess. My teacher, Ms. Prins, saw me mowing too, and I was certain that while she never had the courage to bring it up, she thought very highly of me as a result. We all knew it was a big deal. *I* was a big deal.

The next year, front yard responsibilities evolved into both front and back, and within a few years I had jobs to mow the neighbor's yard, and then the one next to them. A year later, I had three more yards. For many summers, I was busy most days for at least an hour or two, walking countless miles behind our rear-bagging, self-propelled, Toro lawn mower. I made a lot of money with my little business and along the way, I converted many pairs of retired basketball shoes into green-toed cast offs that my mom didn't really want in the house. Mowing was part of my life, and I was good at it.

My favorite lawn to mow was our home yard. I knew every nuance, every bump, and every tree root. In order to keep the yard from developing wheel ruts, I changed the direction of the cut weekly. Horizontal rows this week, vertical next week, then diagonal, then the other diagonal. Eventually, to stave off the monotony of that repetition, I began to experiment with different mowing designs. Sine waves, circles, and even a string art pattern. I stopped short of taking official measurements, but I was willing to add time to the task in order to maintain the integrity of my design concept. It had to look just right. Adding the design was rewarding for me and my dad liked to come home and see what my new creation was for the week. Sure, there were plenty of times where I didn't feel like doing the work, but once I got started, I enjoyed the task, the satisfaction of a job well done, and particularly the aesthetics of my designs. I have to admit it, I kind of liked mowing.

***

Many years have passed, I'm twenty-seven and have my own home, but I still don't mind the task, so as crazy as it sounds, I want to mow my lawn today. I'm even leaving work early for that very reason.

I know what you're thinking. Leaving early sounds like a lame excuse some degenerate makes to get home so he can mow for twenty minutes and then crack a few cold ones with his friends in the garage. That's not it though; I don't even drink. I'm skipping out because I have already put in well over forty hours of billable time at my engineering consulting job and because of two other realities looming in my mind: my yard is huge, and my mower is a piece of junk.

When we bought our house, our first one ever, it was mid-summer, so I needed to get something quickly to address the yard, and I wasn't exactly flush with cash. I ended up getting a mower for free from a friend of my dad who openly warned me that it runs, but it had a few, shall we say, idiosyncrasies. Namely, the pull cord has a mind of its own. You know, that little rope with the handle on the end. It usually pulls out just fine and the engine will start, but along the way, something gets jostled loose, making the rope not quite retract all the way. After taking it apart a few times, I learned that a poor retraction spring was not keeping the rope recoil cylinder taut with the engine interface. The result was every once in a while, the free-spinning piece on top would catch on the rotating components of the engine and produce a shrieking sound. Not just any sound, more like a flock of pterodactyls protecting their young. A series of high-pitched, piercing screams that penetrate to your core. It's a sound you can never forget and one I worked to avoid.

Tactical experiments proved that if I pulled the cord all the way out and held it there, it forced the malfunctioning piece to stay engaged and, voilà, no shrieking. But this ploy leaves me with six feet of cord in my hands and no way to safely mow. I keep imagining if the loose rope were to get caught in the blade, then the mower would slowly eat itself. I'd kind of like to see that, but it seems like a bad idea, so I have learned that if I wrap the cord around the mower's handle cross bar six times, holding it secure with one hand and tying it tight with no slack with the other, I can keep the pterodactyls at bay. Problem solved. Well, not solved at all really, but managed, and I can get back to actually mowing.

Our property is a beautiful flat expanse that backs up to woods and all together, it includes over an acre of grass. I love my yard. I have trained my whole life to mow this yard. I have dreams of a soccer field and a pole barn with an indoor basketball court, but really, for now, I just like the grass. But there is a lot of it.

In addition to being functionally quirky, my mower is also a standard walk-behind model with no self-propelled features and a narrow twenty-two inch cutting swath. That's a lot of lines and a lot of laps. I am twenty-seven, so it's fine, I can use the exercise, and I don't mind walking. It's the time that is the issue. It takes me two hours and forty-five minutes to complete the job, not including bagging, refilling the gas, and manning the quirky gerrymandered jib line on the front of the mower. Nearly three hours from start to finish. In late June or early July, it makes for a long evening of dodging mosquitos at dusk. In any other month, it means getting caught in the dark and leaving the job unfinished, which I hate, which then also requires a two-day deployment. Alternately, I can start early enough that it doesn't get dark before I'm done. Hence, I'm leaving work early.

So now I'm home, I just finished fueling up the mower, strategically placing the gas can for mid-session refueling, starting the ornery beast, and delicately tying the pull cord. I've completed only a handful of passes and navigating the slalom course of pine trees in the front yard, when Kylene arrives home early too. She doesn't have to mow, so I don't know what her excuse is. I wave as she pulls into the garage, but I continue moving; I'm in a race against the sunset. A few minutes later, she comes out the front door to talk to me, a rare occurrence when I'm in the mowing zone, and I'm wondering what she's doing out here. I wave again but she walks right out to me and gestures for me to stop. I pause but leave the engine running.

"What?" I yell over the roar of the mower.

"Can you stop for a minute?"

"You want me to turn it off?" I confirm, a little exasperated. Not because I didn't hear her, I know what she said. I'm clarifying because she knows full well how much I've been fighting with this mower, the shrieking, the tying of the cord, leaving work early, the rapidly emptying hourglass signaling the coming darkness. She's my wife, she knows all of it.

"Yes."

"Ohhhkaaaay," I reply sarcastically, yet begrudgingly, I untie the cord, feed it back into the spring retractor, and turn off the engine. The sudden silence is deafening but refreshing.

"What?" I say again, noticeably interrupted.

"Here," she says, and hands me an envelope.

"What's this?"

"Open it."

"Right now? You had me turn off the mower for this?"

"Yes."

I slide my finger below the flap, open the envelope and find a card inside. On the front is a black and white picture of a doorway with a little kid peeking around the corner. I open the card and see it's filled with Kylene's writing. Still irritated at the mower stoppage, I begin to read:

"Hi Daddy…"

Two words. Only two words into reading the mystery card inscription, and my heart has stopped. That's all it took to alter my life. The rest of the card mentions something about being nice to mommy and when the expected date of arrival is, but I don't memorize those details. I'm still struck by the opening. Hi Daddy. Daddy. I'm bursting. I have never felt so excited that I can't adequately describe this new sensation. I hug and kiss Kylene right in the front yard. Right where our lives were transformed, where everything changed.

I am going to be a father.

Wishful Thinking

Years before, one summer weekend at our family cottage, when I was maybe twenty-four, my older sister Ang had invited her life-long friend, Heather, over for the day to enjoy the lake. Beyond a cherished time for the two of them to catch up, the friends' reunion also provided an opportunity for Ang's young son, my nephew Mason, to play with Heather's two little girls. The kids' budding friendships were also blossoming as he was about four at the time while the girls were four and three. Kylene and I were there too, using the boat, playing trackball on the beach, lounging in the sun, and spending time with family. When we came into the house for lunch, the three young kids were already perched on the barstools at the raised kitchen counter, eating grilled cheese sandwiches, chips, and grapes off paper plates nestled into round wicker holders. I don't know if it was the trio of sun-bleached blonde heads, the many pairs of greasy hands devouring the food, or the collective din of their little voices, but Kylene was smitten by the whole scene, so much so, that she remarked out loud,

"Look at those three, that's what I want right there. Girl, boy, girl."

Ang quickly countered,

"Well, I don't know how you'd do that. These two are the same age," referring to Mason and Heather's oldest, "and she's only a year behind," referring to the younger sister.

Kylene was undeterred,

"Yeah, I don't know, but that's what I want."

It was a nice sentiment, and being so early, only our first year or so of marriage, it was just a rosy thought of a future in which we might be blessed with children. Of course, like Ang had said, it couldn't possibly work out to match the exact six greasy hands scenario currently playing out on the stools, but maybe something, someday.

Premature Departure

A year earlier, as I finished graduate school at the University of Michigan, I had multiple job offers across the state and several more in Chicago. I was twenty-three, done with school, and leaving campus. Kylene, a year younger, had been accepted into her own graduate program at UofM and was staying another year in Ann Arbor. I could have taken one of the jobs in Detroit and been close to her the whole year, but the job I really wanted was in Chicago, and when we talked seriously, we both saw our future together being in Chicago and not in Detroit.

With her important blessing in my back pocket, I took the job, moved to Chicago, and worked there for fifteen months until we got married, after which she moved to join me. We both worked hard, traveled a lot for our jobs, and stayed focused on our careers. We relaxed on weekends, gorged ourselves every Friday night on Giordano's deep-dish pizza, found a church that started at eleven a.m., and slept our way through a lot of Sunday afternoons.

Though we lived in the suburbs, we experienced a lot of big city life. She took the train to the city and had audit clients across the greater Chicago area while I spent most of my days hanging off skyscrapers and inspecting deteriorating facades. We didn't have much, and didn't spend much, but we had each other, and we enjoyed doing things on our own in a big new world. We loved it there.

We didn't love our townhouse, however, even though it was decidedly better than the dumpy apartment I lived in my first year alone in Chicago. It was fine for the time we had it, but it wasn't going to be long-term. I hated paying rent. I wanted to buy something to build equity and I couldn't stand throwing away money so inefficiently.

Convinced it was time for something more permanent, we found a realtor and started looking. We quickly discovered that our budget didn't go very far in suburban Chicago, at least not in any desirable area. Houses were either tiny, dilapidated, or fifty miles from anywhere significant. It became clear that a nicer townhouse or condo were more realistic options. We shifted our search but were not impressed with the condo market either and came away frustrated, feeling sort of stuck. Nothing in our price range seemed worth the cost, but we didn't want to keep renting either. We tabled the idea for six months as we pondered our plight.

I began contemplating bigger changes and eventually proposed a new idea. We had always talked about moving back home to West Michigan someday, but neither of us felt like we were done in Chicago. I began to reason that if we were going to leave anyway, why not just go now? In Michigan we could afford a nice house in a nice area, and we could get started having a family. I wanted to start having kids soon, maybe sooner than she did.

I wanted my kids to know their grandparents. Not just know of them, but really know them as fun, able adults, full of life and personality, not just as old people. Kylene's grandparents had been relatively young, and she has fond memories of time with her cousins and sisters at her grandparents' house. She knew them all so well from her many years of time with them. I was the youngest grandchild on my mom's side and near the end of the line on my dad's side. I loved my grandparents, and I knew them pretty well, but they always seemed old to me. If we waited too long, I was worried the same thing would happen to my kids, just due to my birth order. Conversely, I saw how my parents were with my nephews and niece and I wanted that for my kids - genuine deep connections and relationships. I wanted to go home and start our lives. What were we waiting for?

The proposal wasn't met with immediate agreement. Kylene wasn't so sure, and I wasn't even sure myself, but the more we talked about it, the more it made sense. We decided to explore the options to see if we could make it happen and I quietly started looking for a new job. It took a while, but I had some interviews, and an offer came through. It wasn't a perfect fit, but it served a purpose: it could get me back to West Michigan. Soon, other pieces started falling into place, Kylene arranged a transfer within her company, and I finally told my boss of our intentions. I left on great terms, and everyone knew it was a move about family and about going home.

After a season of hoping and planning, summer arrived, we packed our stuff into a moving truck, and we left, just over three years after I had arrived. Leaving was harder than I had ever imagined. We left a known path of happiness and success, and we did so prematurely, ahead of the schedule I had originally planned. I left behind a job I loved and a city I had grown to understand and appreciate. We traded it all for a large unknown, chasing our dreams back home, close to family, and hoping to build our own family.

Greener Grass

A lot of things brought us back, and now I'm still standing here in the front yard, losing valuable time, but with the two words in that card, suddenly, things on a more distant horizon seem much more important than the waning daylight.

A baby! We planned to start a family soon, but I didn't think it would happen so fast. We haven't even really started trying and this news already? My goodness!

I have always wanted to be a father and now it's happening. My mind swarms with all the things I need to plan and get done before the baby comes.

My test. Oh no, the test. A clamp of worry tightens on my temples. I had been studying since January for the Professional Engineering licensing exam. Weeknights after work were spent at the kitchen table reviewing three chapters per week. Saturday mornings I commandeered a private room at the local library for hours, solving study problems and taking practice exams. The test had encompassed most of my spare time and saturated most corners of my mind. It's almost a rite of passage for most in my field and represents a major steppingstone in my engineering career.

The good news is, I took the exam last month, in April, and I feel like it went well, but the bad news is I don't have the results yet. If I don't pass, I'll have to take it again. That would be disappointing, but manageable. Or at least it would have been. Now, the pressure intensifies.

I do not want to study for another three months and especially not with a baby on the way. I won't have time. I need to have passed that test.

I restart the mower, resecure the cord, and resume mowing, only my toes won't get any greener today. My feet aren't even touching the ground. I'm walking on air and my mind is awash with thoughts, ideas, and questions.

What about a baby name? What will the baby look like? What about our cars, and how do I get infant car seats? I need to finish the landscaping. I'll have to repaint the guest room and make a nursery.

There is so much to do. I don't know if I'll be ready.

Part II - Dreaming

Knowing

There is nothing quite like the feeling of knowing something important. Holding information that others don't have, particularly when it's good, life-changing news, imbues an incredible, electric sensation. The energy feels so exhilarating, and you're so happy about it, that you want to tell the entire world. Most news like this is shared broadly and immediately. I got the job, I passed the test, she said yes, and we're getting married. We tend to share good tidings with everyone we care about and those who care about us. We even share it with people that don't really care because we just can't help ourselves and it spills out in uncontrollable eruptions.

Learning we are going to have a baby is the greatest news of my life, of *our* life, together. I am elated, hopeful, and bursting at the seams. I want to share this joy with the whole world, or at least anyone who will listen. Yet, we haven't told a soul. We are waiting because they say we are supposed to.

I don't know who *they* are, but evidently, *they* advise that you should wait to disclose baby news until you're sure the baby is healthy. I guess this means through the first trimester and past the point of most potential developmental problems. In recent history, we have had family on both sides who had some difficulties in the baby department, and we witnessed firsthand how early sharing of good news can also mean sharing of heartbreak later. I want to maintain control of the circumstances and avoid the possibility of that painful follow up, so we wait.

I'm not sure why I think waiting is better, if it protects Kylene, or if I'm trying to protect my family from the pain of disappointment in the case of something unexpected. Or maybe I'm just selfishly protecting me and my heart. In my engineering mind, this is logical and efficient;

if the joy is withheld and something does go wrong, I can minimize the damage, bury the pain, and no one ever needs to know.

Mr. Roboto

I guess I'm sort of good at that already, burying my feelings, or just not allowing myself to show that I have them in the first place. After all, I am an emotionless robot. At least I've been accused of being such several times. My sister-in-law lovingly bestowed the label upon me in the last few years, and although applied good naturedly, such observations usually hold a kernel of truth. Technically, I think she suggested that both my older brother Luke (her husband) and I were such robots, but I was markedly worse in the non-emoting monster category. She didn't outright say that of course, as she's a lovely person, but I inferred it.

She's not the only one. These accusations are lobbied by others too, and they often come in conjunction with reminders that I, and he, are engineers. Yes, both of us, and for some reason that seems to come up a lot. Unfortunately, the occupational reminders don't include any sense of pride or admiration, like you might expect if we worked in medicine, or were showcasing our (nonexistent) abs as models, or were professional athletes, or had faces (and abs) that looked like Ryan Reynolds. There aren't many positive connotations. Instead, it is merely a dismissive explanation of why we are the way we are. Or at least why we are perceived to be that way. He's an engineer, a.k.a.: cold, unfeeling robot.

All kidding aside, it's probably fair to say she is not entirely wrong. I don't show much *outward* emotion other than adrenaline-fueled elation, or anger and frustration with inefficient or annoying things, processes, or people. I'm a connoisseur of eye rolls and disdainful expressions, but visible signs of empathy, sympathy, and kindness aren't really in my regular rotation. Sentiment, nostalgia, or anything remotely heartwarming - please. Of course, I love my wife and my family, but generally, the bumpers on my bowling lane of life keep me centered on hard work, organization, efficiency, logic, and reasoning. My system programming categorizes expressions of feelings as distractions and indicators of weakness. Frankly, outward feelings are a loss of control.

Granted, these are discernments of my mental status in my late twenties; I was always systematic, but I wasn't always so guarded. It took me years to develop the schematics of my robotic programming and erect all the accompanying emotional barricades.

But how did I get here? If I rewind to when I was growing up, I was no stranger to ridicule. I mean seriously, I had an older brother, so it was just part of life. Don't interpret that too deeply, though. I had a great childhood, with a loving family, and a community of supporting friends, teachers, pastors, Sunday school teachers, coaches, and others. Even so, we are all shaped a little by our original environments and mine seasoned me so that I was never a silent victim. It always came down to asserting control of a situation, establishing order; or at least trying to.

As early as elementary school, I was eternally convinced that I was right on just about everything, so I railed against any circumstance I deemed unfair. When confronted with teasing or anything I perceived as a slight, I counterattacked, spewing verbal venom at my playground assailants. I always sought to control things, and if I saw a problem, I was going to fix it. Even, or especially, if that required me to remind you how I was right.

Despite my relentless pursuit of personal justice, or perhaps because of it, I wasn't always at the top of the elementary school social pecking order. I had plenty of friends, but waging occasional wars of words left me labeled as "defensive" and "can't take a joke," while the popular elite got to remain aggressive, aloof, and basking in the incessant flow of social admiration. That dichotomy wasn't fair, and I tried to control the social narrative to show everyone I was right about that too. But, despite my contesting, I couldn't change the situation, and the unfair, nonsensical social hierarchy remained, confounding me.

In junior high, things got a little worse. I wasn't a troublemaker at all, and I didn't usually start the verbal jousting, but it was rare for me to back down. When challenged or teased, I still didn't accept it good-naturedly. Fighting back against the self-anointed popular crew remained a losing battle, but I wouldn't surrender. Instead, I weaponized my intelligence with sharp words, certain my aggressive responses would gain me respect and junior high social cachet. It didn't. Each occasional instance only caused me to slip further.

Eventually, the pattern reached a crescendo one night at an eighth-grade class party, when a popular classmate informed me,

"We all hate you anyway, why don't you just leave and stay away from us."

I was fourteen and I never saw it coming. Encountering a reality I couldn't control, my fragile junior high existence unraveled in a matter of seconds.

He didn't speak for everyone, but I believed he spoke for most, and for the first time, I just took it, and I left. First the party and then the social circles entirely. I found acceptance in the grade above me. I still went to school, remained engaged with my teachers and stayed at the top of my class academically, but socially I kept my head down and my mouth uncharacteristically shut for several months.

As I recovered, I reassessed and tried to regain control of my circumstances from every angle. I refocused on my natural engineering tendencies—ones I didn't even know I had—and programmed new rules and methods: not *always* saying what (I thought) needed to be said, and internalizing feelings—preventing them from surfacing. Instead, I navigated difficult circumstances through mental focus, compartmentalization, and a refusal to outwardly reveal any weaknesses.

In hindsight, I now realize as I stood vulnerable on the doorstep of adolescence, the social sequence broke me in ways I didn't understand. I never fully came back from that. Not the same at least.

My early teenage psyche thought I was developing internal strength, but my rewired processing manifested in myriad ways, some unhealthy. I turned the brokenness into unspoken fuel for an already raging fire of perfectionism. I strived to be better than everyone at everything just to prove that I could outdo them. All of them. I buried any emotions I had and allowed, or maybe forced, myself to harden.

By the next fall, my plans seemed to be working. I had cut my glorious nineties-era mullet (you're welcome, ladies), I had physically matured, and many of the troublesome classmates had transitioned to a different school. I was fifteen, the president of my class, the captain of every team, and a lead in the school play, but I was still guarded with my artificial emotional armor.

Just as things seemed to reach a peak of improvement, a cherished teacher and family friend was unexpectedly lost, upsetting my newly regained equilibrium with yet another event outside of my control.

It shook me. I had encountered death a few times before—namely my great grandparents—but this loss was the first time I experienced something sudden, unexpected, and proximate. Everyone asked and I always said I was fine, but I don't think I was. Shock, confusion, and unprocessed grief swirled, but my internal control manifests didn't allow for exposure of such things. Instead, the emotions were filtered and pressed into new layers of lacquer, adding to my hardened, glossy finish. Meanwhile, as the elected head of the oldest grade, I was asked to speak at the school memorial service. I didn't show an ounce of the pain I was harboring. I was ice cold; robotic even.

Fast forward back to my twenties, after more than a decade of practice with this stoic demeanor, my controls and repression skills are finely tuned. I'm really good at it, even when I shouldn't be doing it. So, while I'm thrilled by our amazing news of pregnancy, with potential pain on the horizon, the subconscious protective programming kicks in and I'm able to squish down all the feelings while we wait. It's the smart thing, the logical thing, for everyone. At least that's what I tell myself.

For Someday

When I was in college, sometime in the months while my sister Ang was pregnant with Mason, my dad decided to build him a cradle. It was hand-made, consisting of end panels and rails fashioned out of oak with decorative scrolled features and a series of thin spindles circumscribing a small flat enclosure where a baby can lay on a special mattress. By any account, the handiwork was beautiful, but it was extra special because Dad made it, for Ang, for her baby, for their family, and it was something they could always keep. Five years later, my brother Luke and his wife were expecting their first child, and Dad began working on a cradle for them. Kylene and I were newly married and living in Chicago, but we were not expecting. Nevertheless, Dad felt it would be most efficient to just make a cradle for us at the same time. No pressure or anything.

With this objective in mind, one weekend when we visited home Dad requested that we accompany him to the local paint store to select a wood stain for our cradle for our baby that we weren't expecting. While in the middle of choosing, my former high school choir director and her husband entered the store seeking paint for a weekend project.

When she asked what we were doing at the paint store, I sheepishly explained about my sister's cradle, and then about my brother and his expectant wife, and that though we were not expecting, we were picking a stain for our cradle that would be for... for…

"Well, for someday," I stammered.

In my head it seemed a little silly, a lot presumptive, and if I were superstitious, perhaps a little reckless to be planning for a baby that wasn't even conceived, for whom the notion of conception wasn't even conceived. Despite my awkward delivery, she didn't think any of that. I could tell she thought it was all just wonderful.

"For someday," she repeated, beaming at me.

Appointments

Our someday has arrived. It is still in the early weeks, and no one knows about our covert baby growing operation, but after a phone call to the doctor, we embark on the first phase of our journey as newly expectant parents: the prenatal doctor appointments.

Today marks seven weeks and we meet at the doctor for some exciting scheduled events—we are supposed to hear the heartbeat. Friends in the past have told me what it sounds like, but I don't exactly know what to expect. I just know I'm hopeful everything is okay, and I'm curious and anxious to hear something.

We are led into a room, Kylene's un-showing belly is smeared with the conductive blue jelly, and the equipment is deployed. There isn't much of anything to see, I feel like we are a family in the 1950s, gathered around the radio, waiting to be mesmerized by an audio-only interaction.

And then, it begins. There are no thumping or thuds, what I'm hearing can be best described as a short, repetitive "whooshing" sound. Whoosh. Whoosh. Whoosh. It's fast, almost airy, and makes me think of fluid flowing through a vessel. I suppose that is exactly what I'm hearing, but it's still not quite what I had imagined it would be. Whoosh. Whoosh. It's incredible.

I wasn't prepared for how overwhelmingly real the audio would be. At-home pregnancy tests are usually reasonably accurate, and even the blood work conducted at the doctor's office is dependable, but those are really just a bunch of magical colored sticks and words on a piece of paper. None of that was compelling evidence, but for some reason this whooshing is strong confirmation for me that this news is indeed real, my baby has a heart, and it is beating or whooshing or whatever that sound is, and I can hear it. *I can hear it!* There is another human forming inside Kylene, and I can hear him (or her) in there. This realization is so amazingly bizarre and yet so wonderful. I can't help but smile and if they would let me, I could sit here all day and listen to my baby's whooshing heartbeat. This evidence is real. This is actually happening.

Sorrows and Joys

We are still waiting to tell anyone. All the waiting means pushing the envelope of excuses as to why Kylene won't participate in many of her normal activities. Mine is a family of avid waterskiers, and Kylene has blended into our morning skiing routine since early in our dating. But this year, since we learned our exciting news, for at least a month of summer weekends she has dodged her turn to hit the water using complaints of the lake being too wavy or that she's too cold. I think my brother is starting to notice.

At a family outing with her side of the family, Kylene's dad arranged for us all to enjoy a high ropes challenge course together. Usually up for adventure of all types, Kylene exaggerated her fear of heights to bow out of the festivities. We wait and keep sliding by, just under the radar, and seemingly free from overt suspicion, but I don't like the lying.

We are getting close to the safe gestational timeline, when the experts, or *they*, say it's okay to mention the news in public. That will be a relief, I'm tired of all the secrecy. When we are alone, we talk about the baby all the time and now, as the weeks have gone by, we finally start flirting with the idea of telling other people. Maybe someday soon, but for now we wait for some inclination of when the time is right. We want the perfect occasion when much of the family is together. I didn't anticipate how the timing would eventually align.

***

My Grandma Workman, my mom's mother, passed away somewhat unexpectedly, around the tenth week of Kylene's pregnancy. In her late eighties, Grandma's health was less than perfect, and having lost my grandpa to a battle with Parkinson's disease over six years earlier, she was lonely and hadn't really been happy for quite a while. We can say all the right things, and that she's in a better place, which we steadfastly believe, but even still, it has been a bit of a surprise. While she could be pessimistic, and as my uncle, her son, described in the eulogy, a touch judgmental, I still remember her warmly.

From the aromas of Thanksgiving dinner wafting through her immaculately clean house, to the box of Bugles corn snacks stashed in her cupboard, to the lyrical rhythm her voice took on when she read the Bible for devotions after dinner, she was a quintessential Grandma, a lasting icon of the family, and an important foundation in my life. She was also my last living grandmother, and she herself was the youngest and last survivor of ten children, so losing her was the end of several legacies. Needless to say, despite her age, her health, and her occasionally prickly demeanor, it still hurts. It hurts all of us, but it is particularly painful for my mom.

The visitation and funeral proceed without complications, and the gatherings afford us all a chance to say goodbye and to reconnect with some of our cousins we don't see very often. With the services concluded, my mom invites the immediate family—me and my siblings, our spouses, and the three grandkids—over for Sunday dinner. We've all accepted the invitation and are reconvening at the cottage after church to enjoy the meal. Kylene and I head upstairs to our seasonally assigned room to change out of our church clothes when I hatch an idea.

"Let's tell them about the baby," I suggest. Selfishly, I want to tell them because we've been waiting, and I'm excited, and I want to tell *someone*. I also want to share it with my family because I'm the youngest, both my siblings now have kids, and I oddly feel like this revelation will complete some larger cycle for us where we've all evolved into parenthood. Beyond my own desires, I am thinking about them too. I have the sense our news will bring some unexpected joy into a weekend dominated by mourning. I'm suspecting this news could be particularly helpful for my mom and hopefully bring a glimmer of light into an otherwise darkened day. Kylene agrees, maybe not with all the reasons careening around inside my head, but with the notion of telling the family, as it is indeed nearing the right time.

We sit down to our typical family Sunday meal when we are together. Mom has prepared a beef roast with gravy, mashed potatoes, corn, cooked carrots, and dinner rolls. There is always too much food and I always tend to overindulge, but it's a great meal and it delivers all the trappings of comfort and family, just as Mom intended.

At some point during dinner, I decide to slip a hint of our news into the conversation. I don't know why I do this sort of thing; I think it's a little bit of grandstanding, but for some reason I come up with these ideas even if they are very un-engineer like. I guess I like to have an entrance, a moment, and a bit of a small spectacle, something memorable. Maybe I just like surprises. That is not true, I don't like surprises. Maybe I like to deliver surprises? Or perhaps I just like setting the scene for a good story to tell later. I'm usually not one to constantly draw attention to myself, but in big moments, I guess I do.

Since our move back from Chicago about a year ago, some of our collective stuff—clothes, books, bags, furniture, memorabilia—has spent some time in storage purgatory. First it lived in Kylene's dad's spare storage trailer, and then some resided in my parents' basement, and then, when we bought our first house, most of it transitioned into my basement. Despite now owning my own personal junk repository, some of my other accumulated things, items which I didn't immediately need, remained in their storage areas, waiting to be rescued.

Each time my parents visited us at our new house, my mom would come with more of my stuff that she was graciously, but deliberately, purging and forcing me to deal with. One time it was all of my old Lego sets, and the next month it was my fourth-grade leaf collection with the catalpa leaf still dwarfing its page and sticking out in all directions. Stuff. Sometimes it was good stuff that I want to keep, and sometimes it was junk I should have discarded years ago. Regardless of actual value, it came, and slowly but surely, like a smuggling mastermind, my mom was cleaning her basement and cluttering mine with treasures of my past. Amidst my archived pieces remaining in storage was a custom, hand-crafted piece of furniture that I had never needed. Until now.

Enacting my plan, between bites I mention casually, "Hey Dad, next time you bring a load of stuff to my house, can you bring the cradle?"

I stopped and waited for an eruption of joyous approval. It didn't come. Instead, I am met with a momentary gap of silence, though two people at the table understood immediately.

"Sure!" he enthusiastically responds, with a smile on his face and tone of voice indicating he understood my meaning.

My mom looks up from her plate of food, ignoring me altogether, and stares straight at Kylene.

"You're pregnant."

It isn't a question, it's a statement, one made with excitement behind her eyes and a catch of hopefulness in her voice. As Kylene nods and smiles, a light sparks inside my mom and seems to melt away a few layers of pain. Pain from the last week, from the last many months, and from the many years of stress of worrying about and dealing with Grandma. It was the moment I'd hoped for, a buoying of her spirit, with a new promise of life to look forward to.

The rest of the family quickly realizes what I have said and joins the chorus of congratulations, all of us enjoying the wave of happiness and kicking off a new season of expectations. The excitement continues and we all start talking over each other, discussing the details of due dates, possible genres of names, and the many things we now get to plan for and dream about.

Amidst the new surge of energy, my parents share a knowing look across the table and though they too exude our collective joyful glow, there is something else in the air. Something unexpected. An exhalation of sorts. I barely notice it and certainly can't explain it, but before I give it any further thought, Dad pipes up and unloads a story none of us had ever heard before. At least no one except my mom.

"Well, now we can tell you," he confesses. "Ever since you broke your leg, we've been worried that you wouldn't be able to have kids."

Those Are the Breaks

Ah yes, my broken leg, one of the classics. It's funny how some of our life anecdotes stay with us and keep cropping up, again and again, in various contexts.

Breaking my leg was one of the most prominent benchmarks of my young life, a clear delineation for my imprinted memories. I can remember some things before that, but I remember almost everything about that experience, and most of my life after.

One fall afternoon when I was four years old, one of Luke's friends pulled a seemingly harmless prank in our backyard. The friend shall remain nameless in this account, but trust me, I know exactly what his name is; it shall never be forgotten. He-who-shall-not-be-named held a length of rope with a loop and slipknot in the end. His intent was to get me to step in the loop, he'd pull the rope, I would fall down, and hilarity would ensue. A silly forced pratfall. He asked me to step in the loop, and being four, I agreed. He pulled the rope and the plan immediately eroded.

The yank of the rope played out just precisely wrong and I ended up on the ground in a heap of screaming, tear-streaked, and snot-covered humanity. Specifically, I ended up with a displaced fracture in my left femur, which paved the way for multiple weeks of traction in the local hospital, months of a full leg cast, and unprescribed restorative physical therapy by way of riding my Big Wheel around the neighborhood.

Unscientific anecdotes like to suggest that your femur is the hardest bone in the body to break. As it turns out, it isn't that hard. I was just standing there one moment, and the next I was on the ground, and I couldn't walk. It seemed pretty easy to me. Anyway, it was a whole ordeal, and kind of a lot for a four-year-old, and I have to imagine it was rather taxing for my parents. The point is, I remember it. I remember a lot of it quite well, and until right now I would have said I remember everything, but the baggage Dad unloads is completely new information.

"What are you talking about?" I ask, genuinely intrigued.

Dad explains. "One morning when I came to visit you in the hospital, I entered your room to discover the nurse technician was in there with the portable x-ray machine. She was taking images of your leg, but she didn't have the lead protection pad over the rest of your body.

"I asked the technician why she wasn't using the pad and she complained it was all the way downstairs on the other side of the hospital. Basically, it was a long walk, and she was too lazy to go fetch it. We had an argument because I made her stop and told her to go get the lead apron and other protective gear. It happened again on a later day when she showed up without the protection, and again I made her go get it. I reiterated under no circumstances are images to be taken of you, ever, without protection. She was not happy with me.

"I then went and lodged a complaint with the head of radiology and the head of the hospital about what had just happened."

"Dad, wasn't it only the one image?" I contend.

"That's just it, I don't know how many images they took, or if they used the lead apron the other times when I wasn't in the room. I wasn't always there. That machine was pointed at your upper leg and was right next to your crotch (his word of choice). The x-rays could have sterilized you and we had no way of knowing. I was furious. I wanted to sue the hospital, but there was really no path for recourse because everything was unknown. Eventually we just let it go."

Mom interjects, "Ever since then, all these years, we have wondered whether that affected you or not, if something happened to make it so that you couldn't have kids."

"I can't believe this! Why didn't you ever tell me?"

They answer, sort of together, her going first, "We didn't want you to think about it, or worry about it. That could have given you anxiety, and that kind of worry can cause problems in your adolescence, and especially as an adult if you're trying to have kids."

Dad concludes, "For twenty-three years, we didn't know and have worried about whether you would be able to have children. Until today."

I'm startled by this revelation, but I can understand their logic. It undoubtedly would have been uncomfortable to learn about my possible infertility if they had told me in my teen years, and when Kylene and I were first married, they probably didn't want to burden us with a worry when they weren't even sure if there was a problem. Still, what if there *had* been a problem? What would Kylene have felt? What would I have felt? How would this have changed our plans? It's impossible not to wonder, but I know these questions don't really matter now. We are expecting a baby, and my parents no longer carry a secret burden of concern for me. And as for me, the weight of knowing, but not sharing, lifts, and I bask in the freedom of transparency and honesty once again.

As we all return to the happy chatter around the dinner table, I sense something more in my parents than just their joy over the announcement of a new grandchild. More than anything else, in this moment, they are both awash with a different, more powerful emotion: relief.

Expecting

Even though our planned timeline for revealing the news to my family was pushed forward slightly, it feels right and sets off a chain reaction of sharing with all of our family and friends.

A week later on the next Saturday, we find ourselves across the state with Kylene's sisters to tell her mom of the pending arrival. We present her with a gift revealing the news and she is so thrilled, she is moved to tears, which leads to tears from Kylene and both of her sisters. Lots of excited conversation follows, but thankfully this time there are no great revelations about decades worth of sterility worries.

Only a few days later, Kylene shares the same news with her dad and stepmom back on the west of Michigan. Kylene's dad is more reserved in his response, but it is immediately clear that he is deeply pleased as well.

While both Kylene's mom and dad have grandchildren in their lives from their respective spouses' kids, for each of them it is the first time one of their own children is expecting. It is a rich new blessing for all of us.

Sharing the excitement with family and watching the joyous response after each revelation is pure fun. Personally, I've been pumped up since opening that card in the front yard several months ago, but lately, bringing more people into the circle of knowledge has accumulated more joy and accentuated what I can only describe as a palpable momentum. I think I'm actually getting more excited. I didn't think that was possible. I guess I shouldn't be that surprised, I saw what a new baby did to my family when my nephews and niece came along, we are simply adding more to the joy column of everyone's respective life ledgers.

As we continue our announcement tour, it is making for a most interesting summer. Despite the fatigue and morning sickness for Kylene, it is a season of nearly perpetual happiness, new experiences, and the effervescent atmosphere of anticipation. The reason is simple and seemingly universally understood: a baby is a gift, a gift of life, the most precious of blessings, and everyone feels it.

Beyond the positive energy in the air, finding the posture of expecting is also a new and interesting transformation. I don't mean Kylene's actual posture, or her body shape, although those are morphing almost daily too. I mean our overall collective mentality as first-time expectant parents.

Now that we've been anointed with this "expecting" status, as we move through any given day, it seems that it should be inherently understood by everyone around, that we are the absolute center of the universe. Did you not get the memo? We are expecting a baby, so therefore the world should stop and take notice of this profound happening.

Pregnancy is so commonplace. Literally every person on the planet was once someone's expected baby, but for us, everything is new, every experience is fresh and amazing, and we expect every tiny detail of our journey to be of great interest to everyone we encounter. Every flutter of tummy activity is celebrated, every millimeter of belly expansion is measured, photographed, and documented on our family blog. We are young, this status is new, and we feel extra relevant and immensely special.

I am just enjoying it, blissfully unaware of just how ensconced we are in our own circumstances. Our exuberance may be a bit tiresome to those around us, but even if they are annoyed, I bet they understand. And even if they don't, I'm too happy to care. I'm going to be a dad, and everything is going perfectly.

Part III - Preparing

38

Grandma's Blessings

I was blessed to have four wonderful, loving grandparents. Remembering Grandma Smith, my dad's mother, conjures up many rich memories, but the two themes that remain most vivid in my mind are the endlessly positive affirmations she heaped upon me and my brother, and how she always gave long, satisfying back scratches.

That may seem a silly thing to mention, but from as early as I can remember, if I sat down next to Grandma, it usually initiated a loving scratch of my back. As far as I could determine, the scratch had been a go to desire of my dad since he was a little boy. I don't know if Grandma started scratching his back and he learned to like it, or if he was always asking her to scratch because he was itchy or had dry skin or some other epidermal ailment. Regardless of the chicken and egg conundrum of their true origins, those patterns evolved into dad's adulthood, and he still harbors an insatiable desire to have his back scratched, much to my mom's chagrin. But Grandma was always willing to oblige. When I came along as the next generation, she either assumed all little Smith boys had skin irritation, or more likely, just knew it to be a loving gesture.

Beyond the back scratches, all while I was growing up, Grandma was always quick to compliment me. She liked my shoes, my shirt, my new bathing suit, my new haircut; She liked my basketball games, my singing, my burgundy 1988 Dodge Shadow. Whatever I wore or whatever I did, whatever I had or wanted, she liked it. I could do no wrong. She was supportive, encouraging and an unabashed advocate of everything about me.

This advocacy was particularly prevalent when it came to working. Since my dad was a high school teacher and he had summers off, he became a licensed builder to fill the gap and increase his income. Every year he would find a client with a construction project to complete. It started with roofing, renovations, and small jobs he could do alone. With two young sons growing up in his household his prospective labor force increased, and he began seeking bigger jobs. Summer projects turned into building an entire house — either for a client or one to sell on speculation. As a result, Luke and I grew up working construction in the summer. That meant from age twelve and beyond, I was up early every morning moving lumber, framing walls, hanging siding, picking up trash, or whatever task was needed at the job site. We worked hard, we learned a lot, we made good money, we were always tan from being outside all day, and we were strong from pounding nails and schlepping lumber and shingles around a sandy job site.

Grandma had been over the moon about all things us before, but our work launched her further into the stratosphere. Her boys were strong, hardworking, and smart — an unbiased assessment for sure — but she didn't ever stop to consider the slightest possibility of nepotism and certainly never thought to sideline her opinions. As a result, we heard about our greatness every time we saw her. More impactful, every young girl that entered our respective dating atmospheres and had the pleasure of meeting Grandma heard about it too. About how great we were. And they heard it a lot.

"I think these boys are hunks," she'd always say. It was not a discussion starter or invitation for dissent. The proclamation was presented as an indisputable fact from the highest of authorities. Never so much as a whisper of a compliment to the girls, just endless, unsolicited confirmation that they were dating the best there was. Her crusade was relentless and though terribly subjective, it was honest, consistent, and arguably, effective. Well, I don't really know if it helped sway anyone or not, but it probably didn't hurt. I have to admit, it always felt good for Kylene, who I never deserved, and we all knew she could have done better, to be occasionally reminded that I wasn't half bad as an option. I mean, seriously, Grandma just said so, didn't you hear her? It must be true.

As the years of our courtship progressed, it became clear that Kylene was sticking around, (likely in no small part due to Grandma's overtures), and we got engaged. My brother Luke and his then girlfriend (now wife) Bridget, had also become engaged a few months earlier. Satisfied her campaign of compliments had concluded in a series of victories and yielded two new granddaughters, Grandma's focus subtly shifted. Being in her twilight years and slipping into what some might have described as early onset of dementia, Grandma deftly transitioned from grandson propaganda into prognostication, particularly on one subject: Babies.

For some important context, we should rewind briefly to 1953 when Grandpa and Grandma Smith were expecting their fourth child, a bit of a surprise tag-along, a full seven years behind my dad, who had been their third. The surprises doubled on February 14, when Grandma unexpectedly delivered two babies, a boy, and a girl. This surprise set a course for the remainder of Grandma's life. Five children, including twins, was a lot to manage and frankly, it had lasting impacts on my dad, his older sisters and of course, on Grandpa. Having the twins was a defining moment for their family, and as such, it bubbled to the surface of conversation more often than you'd expect. The twins this; the twins that; when I had the twins; when the twins were this old. The twins' arrival, and everything that changed afterwards as a result, became the backdrop to the stories we heard Grandma tell time and time again. Stories marked by surprise and hardship, but also marked by a sense of triumph and overwhelming love.

Grandma often injected her personal backstory when talking with her granddaughters-in-law, Kylene and Bridget, at Thanksgiving, Christmas, or summer family gatherings. Specifically, Grandma began vocalizing what I think was a hope of hers, but she presented as more of a prediction,

"One of you girls is going to have twins."

She uttered the phrase, not once, but quite often, and repeatedly. She wasn't joking. Of course, neither of the girls was a blood relative of hers, and scientifically speaking, any hereditary tendencies toward twins follow the eggs, and therefore the mother's line. Certainly science, genetics, and statistics did not support any of Grandma's intuitive claims. Nevertheless, she persisted.

"One of you girls is going to have twins."

Bridget was usually quick to politely decline such a generous blessing, and she and Kylene chuckled and wrote it off to another thing Grandma tended to repeat.

Despite a steady decline of her health and her slowly decreasing lucidity, the conversation continued for years, and she remained steadfast to her twin proclamation.

The fall after we moved back home to Michigan, Grandma sadly succumbed to what she called "the C word." It was expected, but still hard to watch my dad suffer through the loss. After a nice service, the various flower arrangements gifted in her memory were distributed to the family. Kylene and I chose to take home a peace lily, a fitting symbol by which to remember Grandma.

Though future decades of our married life would prove houseplants do not fare well in the Smith abode, the peace lily confronted and confounded those odds by thriving as it stood proudly on our fireplace hearth. It flourished so much that it began to outgrow its container. I did what any seasoned (or imposter) gardener would do: I split the peace lily. What had been expected to be one, was now two. Double blessings from Grandma.

Just to Rule it Out

Around seventeen weeks, we head into the doctor's office for another appointment. We get to hear the baby's heart again and go through the litany of questions concerning prenatal care. The doctor seeing Kylene is Dr. Bateman (not her real name), an obstetrician/gynecologist who previously practiced where we grew up. Luckily, even though we are relatively new to the greater Grand Rapids area, she has been Kylene's doctor since high school. We have seen her on previous appointments, and she's been around quite a bit, so we are all already comfortable with each other.

After completing the standard form of questions, Dr. Bateman keeps right on talking. She is always so pleasant and even though it's probably a daily routine for her, she lets us glow in the novelty of our first pregnancy. She even seems to genuinely share in our excitement. We all keep talking while she makes some final notes and then starts to wrap things up. As she finishes, Dr Bateman measures Kylene's pronounced belly from top to bottom—below her chest and past her belly button to her waistline. Then she measures from side to side, again up and over the belly.

"How many weeks along are you?" she lightly queries, barely interrupting the cordial conversation.

"I think about seventeen weeks," Kylene responds. She measures again and writes some more things down.

"Hmm, huh." She pauses pensively for a moment and then exclaims, "I'm going to run down the hall and see if the ultrasound room is available. I'm hoping we can get you in quick just to rule out multiples."

And she leaves.

Her words hang in the air of the small exam room and the two of us are left just staring at each other.

"What did she just say? Rule out multiples?" I ask, making sure I understood.

"There's no way, there's no way. She said just to rule it out," Kylene replies, ever so calmly.

In my head, I'm self-regulating.

Ok, if it's just to rule things out, and it gets us an early ultrasound to see the baby today, then that's a nice surprise for this appointment. All good.

Dr. Bateman returns with news: they can fit us in for the quick ultrasound. She leads us down the hall and ushers us into a larger room with a reclined bed, a large monitor and ultrasound equipment, where a friendly young woman who will be our sonography technician awaits our arrival. As the tech prepares the equipment, Dr. Bateman provides some quick context regarding the purpose of our unscheduled visit to this particular room.

"Mom is seventeen weeks and measuring a little bigger than I expected, we just want to take a quick look and rule out twins."

"Ohh, I'm a twin," the tech happily announced, "that would be exciting."

She and Kylene strike up a friendly chittering as she sets things up, and after a quick warning that it might be cold, the tech smears the conductive blue gel on Kylene's belly. The tech positions the receiver on the belly and starts the exam with her eyes on the screen, all while keeping up the friendly chatter with Kylene.

"Well, two is better than one, right?"

"Oh, sure. Haha," Kylene responds casually.

But what Kylene hears as nothing more than a rhetorical question, a simple back and forth, I quickly realize is an exclamation. The tech is staring at the screen and so am I, intently, and wide-eyed as I'm processing what she actually said. Granted, I'm not a certified sonographer, but I don't have to be. I can see things very clearly. One circle - head. Another circle right next to it. Another Head.

I firmly interrupt Kylene's banter. "You're not understanding what she's saying." My tone is not calm, nor kind.

"What do you mean?"

"Look at the screen!"

Kylene turns her head to finally look at what the tech and I are seeing on the screen and her face reveals she has now caught up to the realization I reached eight seconds earlier. There are two babies.

Sensations and Superpowers

You might not remember the sensation at that moment, but if you were anywhere in the Midwest region, you likely felt it—the tear in the time-space continuum that occurred. There was an electromagnetic pulse that pierced through our existences. No physical damage occurred, the power stayed on, and the rest of the world kept spinning, unaffected. It was brief, so you might have missed it, but trust me, it happened, and our world was permanently changed. The glimpse of those two heads created an instantaneous shift, transforming us from excited, organized, continuously planning twenty-somethings to trembling piles of confused, terrified, utterly overwhelmed, goop.

There are two.

Oh my gosh, oh my gosh, oh my gosh…there are two. There are two! How did this happen?

I mean, I know how it happens, but this, twins, doesn't just happen.

What if, holy moly, Grandma Smith's twins and her premonitions, and the peace lily that I split into two, and the x-rays… the x-rays!

The x-rays when I broke my leg. They definitely didn't sterilize me, and now there are two babies.

The x-rays gave me superpowers!

Surely this is the most plausible explanation for fathering twins. Perhaps this is my long-awaited comic book superhero origin story? Or maybe it would be best for me to revisit the theory later when my mind is a little clearer. For now, superpowers aside, I can barely contemplate the proof in front of me.

There are two babies. There are two babies. Two. Babies. We are having twins.

Once the universe resumed and time restarted, tears erupt from Kylene. Not sad tears, but tears of disbelief, excitement, happiness, and surprise. Tears of being scared, of being sick to her stomach, tears of how are we going to do this? All of those; all the tears. I am more characteristically stoic, but my internal fire is broiling, and my mind is redlining at unhealthy levels. I had been so self-assured, so calm, so ready. I had a plan, I had it all under control, and now all that is suspended and replaced with abject fear.

What are we going to do?

Doubling Down on the Deal

The bubbly tech interjects yet again, "Would you like to know the babies' genders?"

I chime in immediately, still wide-eyed, and now staring at Kylene, "Remember our deal! "

The deal. I had forgotten about the deal! Since revelation day when I was mowing the lawn, Kylene had been adamant that we would not find out the gender of the baby before the child was born. I had been in strong disagreement and wanted to find out. She wanted it to be a surprise, while I contended the information is a surprise whenever we find it out, so waiting until the baby is born only delays the surprise. The timing of the receipt of knowledge doesn't change the joy of the knowledge, I reasoned. I felt we should enjoy the surprise now and then we could plan and purchase things accordingly. It only makes sense. Any logical person would agree, and we are logical people so that's what we're going to do. Case closed.

It turns out I was wrong, and the case was very much not closed. I volleyed a series of options on how we could get it written down in an envelope so we could open it and find out when we were ready. Or how I could find out and she wouldn't find out and I just wouldn't tell her. She was really not a fan of that particular suggestion, and I lost considerable points in the great scorebook which tallies instances of husband idiocy. (Husbands: If this is the first you're hearing about the book, go ask your wife. You're in it.)

There were many more ideas proposed, each more convoluted and pathetic than the last, and each just as unsuccessful as the first, with none of them making a dent in her resolve. My salvo of deftly crafted negotiations was legendary, it would have impressed Henry Kissinger, but in the end, there was no movement. We were not going to find out the gender. Case closed, again, and for real this time.

Slinking away from the battlefield, as a last feeble attempt at salvaging at least a shred of dignity, for some unknown reason I lamely tossed a bizarre hypothetical situation on the table for consideration. What if we happen to have twins, then, *then*, we should absolutely find out.

Whether exhausted from the exchange or stunned by the sheer absurdity of the posed situation, Kylene had agreed. She agreed that if that ridiculously unlikely event came true, then yes, we could find out the genders of the babies. BOOM! Score one for me in the victory column.

In hindsight, especially in this frantic moment in the ultrasound room, having previously negotiated a corollary amending the decree from the queen seems like a stroke of genius. What foresight, what prescient awareness of my wife's subtle situational physiological nuances. I was so aware and in tune with everything that I had known, *somehow,* I had known what was coming and had set up my argument perfectly. It makes sense. Of course I knew, I'm an engineer.

Sadly, none of this speculation is true. We had no relevant family history or other reason to believe twins were in our future. We simply had a bumbling moron, excited to be a dad, who desperately wanted to know if he was having a boy or a girl, grasping at straws and making last minute overtures to accomplish his goal. I didn't know anything, and unlike Grandma, I wasn't predicting anything. It was just pure, pathetic luck. Or superpowers. Either way, it happened, we had the conversation, she agreed, and now I am enacting the deal clause and forcing a tectonic shift in posture on the topic.

"We are finding out! You said!"

She really doesn't want to find out but now I am the one who is adamant. "We don't need any more surprises; we need to know."

Miraculously, she acquiesces. "Ok, I guess so."

Despite the rousing rally of agreement, I take her begrudged acceptance as a win and confirm to the tech,

"Yes, we'd like to know."

The tech immediately obliges and refocuses our gaze to the screen so she could commentate and share the information that she already knows.

"Here is Baby A and she is a girl."

A girl! A girl. We are having a baby girl. My heart floods with waves of protection and love, feelings connected specifically to my girl. I am going to have a daughter.

I barely have a moment to comprehend this amazing information when she continues,

"And let's look at Baby B," she narrates as she repositions the device. "Baby B is a boy."

A boy! My heart floods yet again with new feelings of pride, strength, and legacy.

I'm going to have a son. A son! A son and a daughter. A boy and a girl, one of each.

I don't remember the next few minutes but somehow in our shell-shocked state we find our way back to Dr. Bateman who does exactly what we need. She explains everything. She explains how we are now considered a high-risk pregnancy, but she also offers calm, positive input and starts to outline the direction of the new plan. More visits, more ultrasounds, and no more seeing anyone else in the office. No nurse practitioners or physician assistants. All appointments are with her. She's in with us, all the way, and it's going to be okay. We're all going to be okay.

If you say so.

New Revelations

We step out of the doctor's office into the bright sunlight of a beautiful late summer afternoon, still reeling from what we just learned. We had driven here separately as we had both come straight from work. We also had plans to meet up with our friends Adam and Kim for dinner tonight.

Still standing there in the parking lot, both our minds shrouded in the enveloping fog, Kylene and I both have the same thought — should we cancel our plans? After all, the entire world has just changed. We are having twins. Two babies at once. Surely no one on earth has ever experienced this level of blessing mixed with anxiety. We should probably just go home and… and do what? Sit there and think about our situation? Stew over and worry about it? We decide there is plenty of time for that later. Life must continue, and we still have to eat. Let's go to dinner.

As we part and get into our separate vehicles, she breaches the other subject on both of our minds.

"Are you going to call your parents?"

"I was planning to."

"Good, me too." And with that, she gets into her treasured black Volkswagen Jetta, her cell phone in hand.

I follow suit and get into my truck. A black 2005 Chevy Colorado with full crew cab and the Z-71 suspension and sport package. We just purchased the truck in the spring, and it is our first brand-new car. Until moments ago, I loved this truck, I was proud of it, and blessed to be able to afford it. Since Adam and I had planned to go for a paddle before dinner, mounted on top is my new kayak, which I had also bought in the spring. A Perception Carolina 13.5-foot kayak, with the hull coloring featuring half yellow and half red. I loved that kayak too, especially how it looked perched on top of my truck, snugly secured with brand new blue ratchet straps, ready for deployment. I like the gear rig so much I have it on my work computer.

A few short months ago, these had been the things bringing excitement to my life. Dumping my kayak in the Rogue River, exploring the waterways, enjoying time outdoors. Then Kylene gave me that card and everything changed. What is important has changed, what I am excited about has changed. We were having a baby, and now this news, today. Twins! Everything has changed again.

Sure, I still like my truck and the kayak, but they don't make me feel the way they used to. Life has gotten really, really, real, and really fast. It had been exciting before, expecting one baby, and now, honestly, it is scary expecting two. Exciting, but scary, but still good. Good news. Beyond good. Incredible.

In our brief encounter in the parking lot, we are still the only ones that know. We are blessed and burdened with once again knowing critical and wonderful information before anyone else. Only this time we aren't waiting, and it is our news to share.

I call my mom, but I can't get through. I don't seem to have her work number handy, and she isn't home yet, so I call my dad, hoping they're together. He answers and in typical dad fashion informs me off where he is and what he is doing. He is sitting on the bench swing at our family cottage with my sister, overlooking the lake.

It seems so fitting that Dad would pick up my call and hear this wonderfully life-altering news while he sits on that swing. The cottage is a cornerstone of our family, a place where my siblings and I grew up in my early years, and then my parents bought the empty lot next door and built a new cottage when I was ten. Various alterations and additions later, it still is a gathering place most summer weekends for our growing extended family.

The cottage is my happy place, where I am most at peace. It is where I learned to swim, to dive, and to waterski. Where I watch early morning sunrises, and ski past dusk in search of flat water. Where I rise early to go for a run around a loop of small lakes that I know by heart. The same route which as a kid I rode my bike with my dad as he ran. The same path I rounded countless times alone or with my brother in an escape of July afternoon doldrums.

Early in our courtship, Kylene visited the family cottage, and she quickly embraced it as well, adopting its importance to me as her own. We even decided to forgo a traditional restaurant setting and held our wedding rehearsal dinner in the front yard. There was catered food and a tent, and it was very nice, but it was simple and casual, and perfect for what I wanted. The event mirrored what the cottage really is: simple, functional, and yet altogether wonderful. It holds a stock of memories in my life that will be forever cherished.

The swing where Dad is sitting now is a chain-suspended bench sized for three to four adults that my dad handcrafted in 1973. It hung between two trees at the old property and naturally moved to the new cottage to continue its legacy.

The centerpiece of the lakeside yard, the swing presides over the property with an air of authority, longevity, and quiet comfort. My grandparents often sat there when they would visit and watched us as young kids playing in the water. I have sat on the swing many early mornings, eaten countless mom-made lunches with a paper plate perched on my lap, retired there for equally many late nights of stargazing and life contemplation, and made hundreds of visits in between. In more recent years, my parents sit there, most often my dad, surveying the lake, watching his kids skiing and swimming, and taking in a kaleidoscope of blessings that he never expected to have, but for the grace of God and the sweat equity he poured into it, was and is able to enjoy. If our family culture has a designated place of tranquility, the cottage is it.

"We had a doctor's appointment today and found out what we are having." I start, with hints of positivity in my voice.

Ever the interested and involved dad and grandpa, he responds quickly, with anticipation,

"Oh really? What did you find out?"

"We are having a boy," I pause briefly, for dramatic effect, "and a girl."

"Twins?! Wow, two babies. Now that is exciting."

Even though I couldn't see him, just by the tone of his voice, I could feel him smiling. My sister tears the phone from his hands and needs to hear it for herself. Soon after, I get ahold of my mom and tell her the same news. When I call Luke, who has a young son at home, he just laughs and laughs. I'm pretty sure he mentioned he was glad it was me and not him.

I need to talk to Grandpa Smith.

He is my only remaining grandparent and as I mentioned earlier, thanks to the aforementioned surprise of 1953, the only other person in my family who knows what it's like to be the father of twins. I call and he picks up but needs my aunt to help him hear what I'm saying. Aunt Marcia makes sure he got the message, and she assures me he is grinning ear to ear. I imagine that it is a genuinely thrilled smile, but

I'm sure he is also laughing inside, knowing full well the journey we are about to embark upon, and no doubt remembering, as I am, the repeated predictions Grandma had made to this effect.

Meanwhile, Kylene connects a tearful call to her mom, and then reaches her dad and each of her sisters. The word is out, and the momentum won't slow for quite some time. The more people we tell, the more real it becomes. The story is real. This is happening. We are having twins.

Breathing Easy

Part of our initiation as first-time expectant parents is attending prenatal education classes. Our local program is split into two parts. First, a tour of the local hospital. We parade around the various spaces while a guide/nurse provides running commentary, somewhat akin to an audio tour at a museum. This desk is where you check in, this area is where the moms are in labor but waiting for contractions to increase, this floor is the labor and delivery area, this section is the moms' recovery area, and this room is the nursery. Here are the elevators, over there is the cafeteria, the bathrooms are down the hall. It went pretty fast and didn't seem like much, but it is helpful for me to actually see the spaces where we will be. It allows me to visualize the process and understand the organization of the program.

The second part of the curriculum is the pseudo-mandatory birthing education—the quintessential Lamaze class, though it isn't really called that anymore. As we enter the room, it is simultaneously surreal and a bit cliché. If you have ever seen a movie depicting this type of scene, well, it is just like that. We take our place in the circle of expectant parents, sitting on the hard floor but perched on a few pillows. Kylene in front and I'm behind her serving as the literal backstop of support.

We settle into our spots and start to survey the circle of strangers. The group leader is a middle-aged woman with a nursing background of some sort. Her voice is sweet but has an artificial tone of a kindergarten teacher who has taught five years too long. She still seems to care and wants to help but has clearly led the class so many times that her heart just isn't in it anymore. After some welcoming banter, we progress around the circle to conduct the forced introductions, announcing our names, due dates, and other friendly nonessential information.

The personal anecdotes drag on, some much too long-winded, and others a little strange, but eventually we achieve some slow progress around the circle. Finally, our turn arrives. Having been sharing and witnessing the responses to our situation on nearly a daily basis, I know what's about to happen.

Step aside folks, things are about to get a little spicy.

"Hi, I'm Kylene and this is my husband, Ross. This is our first pregnancy, and we are having"- *Wait for it…here it comes* - "twins."

Mic dropped. Now for the fallout, which plays out predictably, since it goes the same way, every, single, time. First, the audible responses. Ooooh. Happy gasps and subdued laughter as if we just dramatically unveiled a new Porsche body style at the auto show. Next, the facial expressions: the smile and nod, the widened eyes of stunned surprise, the look of pity, and of course — my favorite — the faraway gaze of "I'm glad it's you and not me." The same one my brother gave me over the phone.

Then, the ridiculous statements begin.

"Oh, I always wanted twins."

Really?! That's so interesting because we're terrified.

"Oh, good for you, I could never handle twins. I don't know what I would do."

Yeah, we're thinking of flipping a coin to see which one gets cared for on a daily basis.

Of course, I don't say the snide comments out loud. Well, not usually. It's just a little irritating and comical at the same time. No matter the circumstance, the twins bomb has the same results, even at its-no-longer-called-Lamaze class.

Now that we've unnecessarily met one another, I'm ready to get down to business, we've got a class to start, so let's get going already — I want to learn all the details and I don't need to waste any more time.

My philosophy has always been that an informed and prepared student has the best outcome. And I have always thrived on outcomes. It's been my mentality my whole life, beginning in kindergarten and all the way through graduate school. Why be satisfied with an A if an A+ was possible? If I had one hundred percent, I wanted the extra credit. I wanted nothing wrong, ever. Excellence and achievement were expected by me, for me, in everything. It had to follow the plan — always be prepared for what was coming, and always be the best.

My newest academic pursuit of parenting is no exception. To master the challenges of babies I figured I could sort of read the manual before they arrive. So, I have been reading all the latest books. I have learned what to expect when expecting while becoming wise to baby schedules and absorbing the secrets of the baby whisperer. I am determined to be as knowledgeable, prepared, and helpful as possible. After all, there are going to be two of them.

With the books read, and the textbook portion of the academia managed, now I'm eager to begin training in the delivery performance arts and the physical challenge. The breathing exercises — my final preparation. Given who I am and how I am, I'm certain I will play a critical role during the contractions, in the pushing, and in the birth! Of course I'll be needed. I'll be essential. When things get difficult, in my wife's moment of need, I will swoop in and lead the way. The gallant knight Sir Lancelot hastening to aid his beloved damsel in distress.

I listen intently and repeat as instructed as she begins.

"Here we go, together now, Hoo Hoo Hee. Hoo Hoo HEEEE."

I'm getting in the groove, mimicking the instructor, and I think I'm doing it right.

I'm certainly better than that guy over there, there's no question about that.

Perusing the room, I'm pretty sure I'm the best in the class, an A+ rhythmic breather. Hoo Hoo Heeeeeeeeeee.

There is just one problem. Kylene informs me, I'm breathing too hard, breathing too much, and breathing too… by her. Then she reminds me of the one critical thing I had forgotten, one of the cornerstones of our married life — that I'm not supposed to breathe at her, on her, or by her, ever. Not just in the class, not in her general vicinity, and certainly not right by her face.

"But I'm sitting right behind you, what am I supposed to do?" *Perhaps a reflective shield or an elaborate snorkel.* These customized rules make my supportive breathing excellence difficult to demonstrate.

"I don't know, but you can't breathe on me."

Right. Maybe I should just not breathe at all?

It's my fault really, how could I have forgotten? We've been married and slept in the same room for three years. How many times have I been reprimanded for breathing on her from the other side of our king-sized bed? Countless times. You need to turn over. You need to face the other way. You can't breathe on me.

Uh huh. Sorry, I didn't mean to be… alive.

My gallantry has been upended, the chink in my armor has been exposed, and my knightly chivalry has been suffocated. I silently envision a new plan to serve my queen in her hour of need. The breathing will be needed, I'm sure of it.

The Foot

Being pregnant with multiples affords lots of additional attention. Some of that attention is self-inflicted as I tell nearly everyone I encounter that my wife is pregnant with twins. So, it comes up, a lot. The robotic programming allows for exposures of joy, but I still hide all the fears. Together, they're almost all consuming as an expectant father of twins. I'm in a fog of uncertainty, a constant worry stirred with excitement, all seasoned with a dash or two, or ten, of pride. Subconsciously, I think my competitive nature leans in as well, as if to ward off anyone else's personal experiences. Your kid was sick? *Ha. We are having twins.* Colicky baby? *Psh, step aside, we are having twins.* Lost two limbs in battle? *That's rough, but have you had twins?* You get the idea. It's constantly on my mind. And the words and comparisons are constantly entering my head and sometimes accidentally coming out of my mouth.

Beyond the self-created attention, there is also additional medical attention in the form of increased frequency of appointments at the doctor. The high-risk pregnancy label comes with more checkups, which frankly, are appreciated, at least most of the time.

Twenty-one weeks in we are here for yet another visit, this time to do a detailed check of all the baby geography, landscapes, and appendages. After cycling through most of the checklist, the radiology technician pauses on Baby Girl's foot. Something appears amiss. The shape isn't presenting right. The blurry spot we're staring at might be a developmental deformity, something like a club foot. Per the technician, this issue is something we'll have to keep an eye on. Concern alarms ring loudly in my head.

What does that mean? What do we do? How do we fix it?

But she says there is nothing to do now, we'll just wait.

Right, meanwhile I'll dwell with this fear for a week or two and imagine all the worst possible outcomes.

Revisiting the foot on a subsequent ultrasound, we pay a lot more attention to Baby Girl this time around. Now the tech offers,

"Let's watch the foot and see if we can make her move it. It might be just fine, and I might just be scanning it from a weird angle. If she moves it, it's probably totally fine."

What!? Are you serious? Why didn't you say that before? I've been consumed with anxiety over the last week worrying about a life of difficulty, ridicule, and hardships, and you might just need to twist your wrist a little to disprove all of that? Let's get our information in line with reality.

Still, it's a glimmer of hope. We try to inspire Baby Girl, who is still inside Kylene, with her twin brother mashed up tight next to her, into moving her foot. We talk to them both. We gently push on them. We then not-so-gently push on them. We cause lots of hand movement, and the other three legs in there are moving, but the foot in question doesn't budge. The tide of fear slowly rises again and with each passing minute, the bleak reality becomes more clear. She's not moving it and there is something wrong. We will have—she will have—some challenges ahead after birth. My protective nature ignites, and the flare grows within me. I feel frustration and sadness and a mourning for something that hasn't even begun.

The tech tries one more time and very casually, Baby Girl moves the appendage and shows us the full profile of a completely developed foot. Not club, reports the tech, everything looks great. A wave of relief envelopes me. I can feel an immediate physical change, like stepping from a stifling humid summer day into the overly air-conditioned vestibule of the grocery store. The coolness consumes you and makes everything momentarily better, everything is more tolerable, and life is worth living again. My emotional relief was just as abrupt and twice as compelling as this is one less huge thing to worry about. Outwardly, the news registers a smile from me and tears from Kylene. Baby Girl, you could have done that ten minutes ago.

The little stinker just wasn't interested in our timeline, she wanted to do things her way. I'm sure that will be the last time that ever happens.

It's not me, It's Him

A few weeks have passed since the foot adventure and tonight, a particularly unremarkable night, our prototypical evening routine rolls out, much like it has many nights before. As the evening dwindles into dusk Kylene and I settle in together on the living room couch to consume some random television show, feature film, or a sporting event that only one of us is interested in.

We reprise roles in our nightly game of make believe, the one where she pretends to be interested in whatever I'm watching, and we both pretend like she's going to remain awake to see how the show ends, how the movie resolves, or who wins the game. Inevitably, as always, the charade collapses, Kylene succumbs to her drowsiness, and falls asleep, and then startles herself awake. The sequence continues through several iterations, each concluding with a startle more violent than the last. Mercifully, she ends her own cycle of misery, announces she is tired, and heads upstairs to bed to repeat the cycle in a more comfortable environment. I had reached the same conclusion—she's tired— forty minutes ago.

The finale of this evening's sleep/startle sequence notifies me that it's about time for me to start making poor late-night eating decisions. It is almost as if my brain has convinced itself that eating alone makes the food taste better and the calories less impactful. If a bag of Doritos is finished and no one sees it happen or hears the bag get thrown away, did the bag ever exist? Humanity may never know the answers to such mysteries.

Snacks completed; I continued watching the game that is keeping me up much later than it should. It just went into overtime, so it appears I'll be up for a while. Out of nowhere, I have a sudden onset of abdominal pain. Sadly, my many forays into the realms of late-night eating have led to heartburn, stomach discomfort, and other digestive maladies so, unalarmed, I assume the sensation will pass. It doesn't. Instead, the pain increases and focuses to a localized pinpoint, but it is on my back, different from the more usual issues in my stomach and gut area.

Maybe I just have to go to the bathroom and this cramping will be taken care of.

Why of course, how stupid of me. Amidst the discomfort, but now suspecting the simple solution, I make the trek across the house. It is not that big of a house, but given my pain, it feels far. Off the couch, across the living room, through the dining room, through the kitchen to the main floor laundry, which also features the half bath. I assume a seated position and expect to get straight to business. Nothing. No relief, no pain reduction, absolutely nothing. It seems this sure-fire theory may not be the solution after all.

As I sit, perplexed, with frustration mounting, the dull stabbing increases further and focuses more intensely in one defined spot, again more in my back. Then, the sharpness heightens to debilitating. Writhing in my helpless state, pressing into my back with my thumb (because that is sure to help), I begin to consider waking up Kylene.

No, I don't want to bother her, I'll be ok if I just…

Another wave of excruciating agony washes over me, unrelenting. This pain is not a mere digestive fiasco. Something is wrong. Doomsday scenarios begin forming.

Am I dying? I mean, probably not, but maybe? There is certainly something wrong here. I'll just try to let it pass. I'll be fine.

Yet another wave crashes over me, doubling the torment. Suddenly, I'm afraid I'm going to pass out. I even picture myself passed out here, in the bathroom. Kylene would find me on the floor, naked from the waist down, with my pants around my ankles. That seems unbecoming somehow.

Didn't they find Elvis in the bathroom? Yes, I think they did. But he's Elvis, and I'm just… well, I'm not Elvis. I don't need anyone finding me in here.

Inspired to avoid some twisted Graceland nightmare scene, I manage to stand up, pull up my pants, and stumble across the house until I am forced to stop again. First, a series of large exhalations. Hoo hoo heee. I'm kind of an expert in breathing through pain. I took a class, you know. Next, I need to survey the landscape in front of me. An insurmountable impediment. The stairs.

I made it this far; I'll just slowly go up like normal. Hold the rail. Now one foot in front of the other and…

Nope. That is not happening. Walking up those stairs is not permitted by my pain to mobility capability ratio.

Why did we buy a two-story house?! If we had just considered a ranch like I wanted, but no, we just had to have a two-story.

On to plan B which, in its brilliance, ends with me crawling. I'm crawling up the carpeted stairs on my hands and knees. Slower, less steady, and infinitely more dangerous.

How is this better? It seems like it's worse.

I finally crest the top of the stairs and crawl into the bedroom. She's asleep. I pull myself up onto the foot of the bed, knees on the floor, arms on the displaced comforter.

"Can you wake up?" No response.

I try again, louder.

"Can you wake up and help me?"

"Wha… what's wrong?" she responds, confused. "Wait, where are you?"

"I'm down here, on the floor. Something's wrong, I think you need to take me to the hospital." My plea for help, the revelation of my near-certain demise is sure to elicit distraught fear and the most heartfelt expressions of worry, love, and desperation for my survival. I brace myself to console my beloved as she formulates her response.

"Can I get dressed and put in my contacts first?" She queries.

"Um, yeah, well, I guess so."

I'm not exactly being blown away by the level of concern being displayed. I'm dying over here on the floor, I just crawled three hundred feet up a cliff to get to you, but sure, we can wait another five minutes. Take your time.

Soon after, we're in the car and headed to the hospital. For some reason Kylene steers over every pothole and every uneven segment of pavement. Each surface discontinuity jostles the tires and transmits more energy to the epicenter of excruciating torment within me. The blackout level pain resumes as I stare out the window clinging to my sanity.

Fifteen minutes later, we arrive at the emergency room. She has done well, the only thing more expedient would have been coming in an ambulance. We don't even park, she pulls right up to the door. It's the middle of the night, my very pregnant (with twins) wife saunters out of the car and is ambushed by a flurry of receiving nurses and doctors who have clearly ascertained the details of the situation.

"Ma'am, ma'am, sit down in this wheelchair. Let us get you inside," they chime, practically in unison.

"It's not me. It's him. I'm fine," Kylene explains.

The tension lifts, the attention shifts, and all eyes turn toward me. Only they're not filled with care or concern, it feels something more like disdain. I can almost read their minds.

Who is this dope? He makes his pregnant wife drive him to the hospital in the middle of the night? Was he shot? Injured? He's not even bleeding.

Having unloaded her pathetic cargo, Kylene parks the car, while I am relegated to the line at the ER check-in desk. When my turn arrives, I relay my symptoms, am handed a clipboard of forms to fill out, and am told that I should provide a urine sample. Kylene returns and takes the clipboard while I take the specimen jar and, once again, head to the restroom.

I'm scared to go. I somehow suspect this is going to hurt but I summon the courage and go. It's burning and painful, but it's not quite as unbearable as I had imagined. I fill the jar, replace the lid, wash my hands, and then pick up the jar to return it back to the lobby counter.

I've had to give samples like this before, but I never paid any attention to them. For some reason, this time, maybe due to the pain, or just the oddity of the situation, I look at the sample. I look closely. Call it gross or weird or whatever, but I looked. That's when I notice a small particle, like a single grain of sand, with the faintest contrails of blood swirling around it, floating in the plastic jar of my warm pee. *Huh.*

I return the sample and go to the waiting area to listen for my name to be called. As I sit down next to Kylene, I tell her what I just saw and my resulting theory. I think I just passed a kidney stone.

After a long wait, the receiving nurse calls my name. I'm led to an exam area, cordoned off with a curtain, and she asks me to rate my pain level on a scale of one to ten.

"Right now?" I clarify. "About a two."

"What about earlier tonight?"

"That was at least an eight, maybe nine." I feel like ten has to be reserved for something else, pierced by a trident, head severed, something more extreme than my terrible tummy ache.

"Did you happen to look at your urine sample?" she questions, and I don't need to answer any further. I know. She knows. She knows that I know. We discuss the confirmation of a likely kidney stone. Based on the play-by-play she offers; I was passing it from the kidney through the ureter to the bladder at home and in the car. That's the worst part, she tells me. Agreed it was. Once in the bladder, it came out when I provided the sample, but despite public misinformation and all men generally terrified of pain in that particular area, that part usually isn't as bad. That was also true for me. More questions, a few more hours, and a CAT scan later, the verdict remains. I passed a kidney stone, and the scans are clear. I'm lucky, a nurse informs me. There seems to have only been one.

Lucky? I'm having trouble enjoying my good fortune right this minute. I have more questions.

"Why did this happen now? Are more stones coming? Should I do something different?" Surely myriad life changes should be in store to avoid a recurrence of this scourge. Nope.

"It just happens sometimes." Have a nice day.

This explanation is not the profound, peer-reviewed white paper of medical epiphanies I was expecting. No real avoidance recommendations besides the instruction to keep an eye on my pee for a while.

"Um, okay. What does that mean exactly?"

I shouldn't have asked. I am dismissed with a prescription, and a plastic filter funnel. I might have had a single stone, and the scans show nothing in the pipeline, but just to be sure, I'm told I should filter my urine for the next few days. Just hold this giant contraption in front of you and check the screen at the bottom when you're done. Every time you go. At home and at work. Lovely.

You're probably thinking, well isn't that sort of weird? Yes! Yes, it is weird. The funnel is not discrete. It is comically gigantic, as if a group of urologists, unable to contain their repressed giggles over their occupation any longer, came up with this enormous screen funnel just to mess with people in my predicament. I can just see them sitting in a conference room, laughing hysterically about the poor schlub who will just take the thing and do what they say.

There is no hiding the funnel in my pocket, so now as I need to smuggle it into the work bathroom, subtlety is not in the cards. I just opt for a large indiscrete plastic bag. Once in there, it's easy to use, but still, it's weird. It's like panning for gold while standing in the stall, only I absolutely do NOT want to find anything and frankly, if I did, I would certainly not be happy about it. Eureka! Another demonic barbed calcium and oxalate deposit to wreak havoc on my ureter. No, thank you. Luckily, I discover no gold and no stones, so I get to just enjoy a week's worth of sheepish walks from my office to the bathroom with a giant plastic bag.

So, what really happened here? That is harder to filter out. Sympathy pre-pains? Perhaps. Fortuitous practice trip to the ER? I guess so, but did we need to do it at night, with Kylene driving, and me… dying? That seems gratuitous. Do I need to be broken down and humbled? No debate about that, but while it was humbling in the moment, it ended as an ego stroking in the long run. Do you know the highest rated pain endured by humans besides childbirth? Kidney stones. That's right, I'm a warrior. Still, it likely pales in comparison to what Kylene is enduring and what she will endure, but I can't argue with facts. Highest. Rated. It's on the internet, so it's true. Maybe that was a pain rating of ten after all.

She's Not Pedaling

September ushers in our third wedding anniversary, and as we have since our first, we are planning a mini trip to celebrate. It has been just over a year since we moved to Michigan and my, what a year it's been. In that short amount of time, we bought a house, we both changed jobs, we bought a new truck and kayak, and I studied for, took, and passed (phew) my professional engineering licensing exam. Now we are expecting twins. This string of changes and the impending ones around the corner makes celebrating seem even more important and more time sensitive, since life with just the two of us is rapidly coming to a close.

We decide to go to Mackinac Island for a long weekend. Such a trip is more or less mandatory for life here in Michigan, so when I realized Kylene had never been, not even as a kid, and had never even seen the bridge, well, that just would not stand in my book.

My insistence on such matters is not always compelling. There are many cases when things I think are important to see or experience do not even remotely register in the fringes of Kylene's consciousness. This time she surprises me. She really wants to go, and I want her to see the island, so it is easily settled—we are going. Even though Kylene is quite pregnant at this point, and is seemingly always tired, we have many months to go before the big day, and we know it is safe to take a trip.

Friday afternoon, I get the car packed and we begin the long trek north, first up U.S. 131 toward Cadillac and then meandering to I-75 on which we'll continue north until it abruptly ends. Well, the highway doesn't end, but the land does. My MapQuest printout indicates I will either have to exit into Mackinaw City or I can continue north over a bridge. But not just any bridge. This is *the* Bridge. In Michigan, that's all that you need to say, "The Bridge," and most natives understand you're referring to this particular elevated expanse, the Mackinac Bridge.

As I reach the last ten miles of land, I realize I'm anxious because I want to see the bridge. Suddenly, as I crest a rise in the highway, I'm rewarded with a fleeting glimpse of the towers, and I have a sudden rush of exhilaration.

"There it is!" I blurt out, revealing my bubbling excitement to Kylene. The towers in the distance serve as a welcoming beacon, stoically standing guard at the gateway to the Upper Peninsula. Just as suddenly as it appeared, the bridge escapes my view, and I am left with a quickened pulse, longing to see it again. Within ten minutes we are on the bridge approach and now there is no way to not see it. It commands attention as it looms over everything, impressive to most, but mesmerizing to me. Maybe it's just the kid in me, or the structural engineer nerd showing my true colors, but I love approaching, seeing, and driving on the bridge. For me, this alone is worth the trip.

The next morning, we wake up early to catch the first ferry across the water to the historic Mackinac Island. Disembarking from the boat we are caught in a torrent of excited visitors and ride the flow of humanity several hundred yards past all the ferry gangways until the surge deposits us onto Main Street.

The island is a living, breathing time capsule. There are century-old Victorian hotels, shops, and homes lining Main Street, most featuring repetitive exterior colonnades interspersed with large hanging flower baskets. The bustling energy along the street echoes with the inescapable reminder of the most unique and renowned feature of the island: there are no cars allowed. Instead, the streets are lined with bicycles, push carts and other simple non-motorized conveyances. Aromas of Murdicks fudge and freshly made caramel corn waft out into the street, and absent any vehicles, the soundscape is dominated by pedestrian chatter, ringing bicycle bells, and the clip clop of horse hooves on the street pulling carts and carriages.

In an instant, a wave of nostalgia hits me.

The horses! It all rushes back to me as I recall riding in a horse-drawn carriage on the island with my family when I was about eight. I don't remember much about the sites we visited or what the guide said, but as I sat in the front seat of the carriage, the holy grail of young boy life experiences was revealed right in front me and my brother. One of the horses farted and then proceeded to make a large deposit of road apples on the ground. It actually happened, I saw it with my own eyes, and partaking in such a spectacle at such a formidable age, steeped in wisdom and maturity, the event had been the single greatest thing that had ever happened in the history of the world. We had scaled the mountain and reached the peak of hilarity. The moment was so indelibly imprinted into my mind it would forever be associated with the island. That was *my* Mackinac Island moment, where the horse farted. Well, now almost twenty years later, I'm back, and it turns out there is much more to discover here. That said, horses are still indeed a big part of the culture, and yes, they still do their business right in the street. Watch your step.

Kylene and I decide to visit the historic fort, later peruse the main street shops, and end up watching a local craftsman make a batch of fudge on one of the large white marble tables. Watching the fudge process is calming, nearly mesmerizing, and it's almost a required activity when you visit. Beyond enjoying the charms of the streetscape there is something more adventurous I want to try. I start eyeing the bike rental place on the corner. In my trip planning research, there were lots of descriptions about the paved road that loops around the perimeter of the island. I want to ride it.

Kylene, however, is great with child, or technically child-ren, and is understandably reluctant to want to make the trek. I'm not giving up that easily. We settle on a fun idea - we'll rent a tandem bike. It seems like a romantic cliché and maybe a bit silly, but it costs slightly less than renting two bikes and I figure it will let me do a little extra work and minimize her efforts. A win-win.

At the rental counter window, we learn the bike rental is strictly by the hour, and any overage of time is rounded up to the next hour. Fifty-eight minutes? We'll have to pay for just the one-hour rental. Sixty-one minutes, that's over an hour, so it rounds up to a two-hour rental. Prices are a little steep, but we are here, so let's do it. Besides, I reason aloud, we can absolutely bike eight miles in an hour. This will be no problem.

Kylene offers, "We can just pay for another hour, we don't need to rush and worry about it." I swear, sometimes it's like she doesn't know me at all.

"If I'm pushing hard, I can average close to twenty miles per hour on my bike, so I can certainly average eight! We will be fine."

We decide to rent the bike, and I am confident it won't take more than an hour. Mounting our trusty dual steed takes a little coordination, but soon we are off and rolling, me in the front and Kylene in the back, riding counterclockwise around the island.

I quickly realize this machine is not my thin tire road bike, and it has only one gear. Luckily, the inefficiency of the gearing is compensated for by the highly aerodynamic wire basket affixed to the front of the handlebars. Perhaps this won't be as speedy of an endeavor as I had suspected. Within less than a minute, we clear the racket and congestion of Main Street and soon the warm late-summer air is filled only with the sounds of us giggling together at the absurdity of the whole ordeal.

Not far around the bend at the end of town we pass by Arch Rock. We pause and look at it for a few moments, but where most people get off their bikes and explore, we press on. She is not going to walk up those stairs and besides, we have a schedule to keep.

We soon discover many of our fellow tourists, definitely more than I expected, have chosen the same riding adventure. There are not enough people to make things crowded as the road is plenty wide, but it makes for frequent interactions with people, especially since we seem to be moving faster than the others and are often passing them. They clearly aren't on the one-hour timetable I have mandated for us.

For the most part, the people seem to be similar to us, Midwesterners enjoying a unique gem of Michigan. I mention that because it is important to understand that here in Michigan, and many of the surrounding states, there is a decidedly Midwestern mentality. It is different from the northeast, the south, the mountains, the southwest, or California. Some differences are obvious while others are more nuanced and subtle. The Midwest mentality implies people are generally kind and pleasant, even to complete strangers. People usually wave, nod, or otherwise greet one another with a "hello," or "good morning," and use words like "folks."

We Midwesterners also find a way to be helpful, even if that help has a hint of passive aggressiveness lurking in the background. We often feel compelled to alert someone their car tire is flat, their blinker is broken, or other things they may not know. However, the mindset can also erode into other "helpful" observations like telling someone their shirt is on backwards, their grass is too long, or you're out of ranch dressing. Not that helpful.

This folksy phenomenon began to unexpectedly manifest within minutes of commencing our ride. One after another people began to call out to me with notes of what they deemed as necessary enlightenment.

"She's not pedaling!"

I respond good naturedly, "That's ok, she's pregnant."

Soon after, another group reports, "She's not doing anything!"

"Oh, I know, and I don't mind, she's resting,"

It's all true, I don't mind, and I don't want her to do much, or to overexert, or become stressed. I mean, sure, a little pedaling effort would be welcome, but she is tired and is carrying my babies, so she's doing a lot already. I can take care of the transport. I just need to keep our average pace above a paltry eight miles per hour.

Near the north end of the island, about halfway through the loop, we discover a topographical feature I hadn't expected. Hills. Not massive mountains per se, but hills big enough that they require some transitions of effort from a rider in any normal bicycle situation. However, I am not in a normal bicycle situation. I remember our bike has a single gear, which until now had seemed way too low as I cruised the flat edge of the island, spinning my legs off to achieve maximum velocity. But now, suddenly, the single gear is comically inadequate for a different reason, as it is not low enough to comfortably spin up an incline. This mechanical disadvantage is only the first part of my problem. Second, I'm also reminded that my bike is twice as long and heavy as usual, and I am carrying the weight of two adults and two tiny babies. This is a family bike ride, on an unwieldy machine, and there is only one functional motor. Me. I'm the motor, and I'm biking for four.

My pulse quickens as my efforts slightly escalate, but our progress continues nearly unabated. The slope steepens, increasing my power output yet again, but I keep us moving, albeit a little slower.

A brief downhill section offers a reprieve but lasts only seconds before it shuttles me right into the next hill, even steeper than the last. I begin to laugh out loud at the necessary exertion, a sure sign that things are actually getting challenging. I'll admit, this effort is harder than I thought it would be. I'm officially lathered into a sweat now, and as the latest hill combats our momentum yet again, I'm now standing up on the pedals, cranking slower and slower, merely willing my legs to advance a few degrees, gradually coaxing one rotation at a time, just enough to maintain steadiness and some semblance of speed. At the peak of my exertion, but not yet the peak of the latest hill, another fellow tourist levies a new accusation of betrayal,

"Her feet aren't even on the pedals!"

"I know. It's ok, she's pregnant with twins."

This time I'm not telling the whole truth. I know she's not regularly contributing, but I wasn't aware of the extent of her withdrawal from participation.

"Your feet aren't on the pedals?" I ask, lightheartedly.

She confirms with a guilty giggle, "No, they are on the frame. It's more comfortable this way."

I steal a quick glance over my shoulder, and see that she does have her feet up, and is casually leaning back. Comfortable indeed. She is Nefertiti reclining on a luxuriously appointed palanquin, being fanned with large palm branches by various attentive, scantily clad manservants. She catches my peeking, smiles disarmingly, and I'm reminded of how precious my cargo — all three of them — really is, and I'm reinvigorated to continue our trek.

The hills pass, as does the halfway point at British Landing, and now my only remaining opponent is the finish line. We can make it, we aren't there yet, but I know I can make it. My pace quickens as we hit an open stretch and some gentle downhill terrain and soon, we are skirting past the western cliffs and Devils Kitchen enroute to the conclusion of our loop. There are brilliant views of the surrounding Great Lakes to our right while pastoral landscapes and historic mansions decorate the panoramas to my left, but I catch and process only fleeting glimpses as I am distracted by the incessant clock ticking in my mind.

We arrive back to the bike shop with moments to spare. I check back in and return our tandem, feeling victorious; a triumph of thrift and bicycling bravado all with the sweet satisfaction of beating the rental company and not allowing them to separate me and my next twelve dollars. I guess I won, but a knot of regret forms in my stomach as I realize that maybe, just maybe, I have inadvertently sacrificed some things just to make the deadline. A few more pauses, a few more stunning vistas, and other fleeting moments of joy along the way. Nevertheless, in spite of the self-imposed urgency of the occasion, or maybe it was the endless string of informants tattling on my pregnant wife, the tandem excursion mints a new impression in my memory banks. This is my new Mackinac Island moment: the first family bike ride.

Part IV - Trials

Bed Rest

A month or so further in the pregnancy, we head in for another doctor appointment. By this time, we are savvy veterans of the office, VIPs really, as we've been here countless times. Appointments, ultrasounds, more ultrasounds, and lots of status checks. I'm usually able to free up my work schedule, so we are almost always there together, and on most occasions, we see Dr. Bateman directly, just as she promised. Things continue to go pretty well, but I am beginning to understand there is a timeline ticking in the doctor's head. She has kept the idea mostly to herself with only subtle hints of what she has in mind. At today's appointment, Dr. Bateman's plan is unfurled. She is ready to institute bed rest. This idea is new territory for us, but it's not complicated. It means rest. Not necessarily in our actual bed, but no more work. Kylene is supposed to stay home, minimize movement and just, well, rest.

When I say that bedrest is Dr. Batemans plan, I don't mean she has light suggestions or even strong recommendations. These instructions are understood very clearly as just slightly less than demands. What about Kylene's work? Her leave is only twelve weeks. That doesn't matter, the doctor reminds us kindly, but firmly. These are the doctor's orders, and that's just what they are — orders. Bed rest is coming soon, now actually, and not because things are bad, but rather because things are good, and we want to keep it that way. We want to keep the babies inside as long as possible to let them grow and develop. Too much mom activity gets them agitated, accelerates the pregnancy, and causes preterm labor. Simply put, we don't want that. Preterm means preemies: it means tiny babies, the neonatal intensive care unit, and a whole whirlwind scene of strife. We don't need that, so bed rest it is.

Surfactant

Around twenty-eight weeks, we go in for another appointment and ultrasound. The babies are getting bigger, but we are starting to notice Baby Boy is slowing in relative growth. He has been slightly ahead of Baby Girl in size and measurements during most of the ultrasound appointments, but recently she has caught up and surpassed him. Today the heart monitoring also shows some infrequent but concerning heart decelerations on Baby Boy. Things are getting more serious, and Dr. Bateman directs us to go to the hospital.

"You don't need to panic or rush. Just go home, eat some dinner, get your overnight bags, and then head downtown to the hospital."

Right. No need to panic and no need to rush.

Her calmness is helpful but not completely convincing. I'm sorry, but I *am* panicking a little and I'm certainly rushing. My nerves are twitching, and a storm of anxiety is moving in, but the doctor is hopeful that after we get Kylene in the hospital, and monitor the babies more closely, we can calm things down.

I desperately hope she is right and that we are able to calm things down.

I am not ready. We are not ready; the babies are not ready. It is too soon. They can't be born today. It's not in the plan.

Not in *my* plan at least.

That's really the biggest problem for me, I hadn't planned for this trip. I'm a planner, a visualizer. As an engineer, I do my best to understand all the variables and consider all the technical outcomes of a scenario. Then, I prepare accordingly. Sometimes physically, sometimes mentally, sometimes both. I like to know what to expect and then I can prepare for it. A prepared response is a controlled response. Being prepared makes things manageable. It's much harder to manage a scenario when it is unexpected, and the outcomes are unknown. It does not compute well for an emotionless robot who wants control of everything.

We stop home, grab the go bags, and then go straight to the hospital. On the way, we discuss urgency levels and decide I will drop her off at the ER and then go park in what will be a role reversal from the kidney stone escapade. Fortunately, because of that debacle, we know the way and my planning mind snaps into recollection mode. I am comforted by knowing exactly what to do. We also discuss who our doctor will be. Since we just saw her, we know Dr. Bateman is not on call. Instead, it's one of her other practice partners, Dr. Franco. The personnel shift concerns us, but not because he's inadequate, and not because we've heard anything bad about him. On the contrary, he is highly regarded, even by us. We had an appointment with him once previously, and we like him, and we had already secretly hoped that if not Bateman, that he'd be our guy, our second preferred option. Still, he's not her, our partner on this journey, and that is the lone blemish on his otherwise exemplary résumé. At least knowing this in advance gives me time to mentally prepare.

Kylene is admitted and we make our way to a large, private patient room. Recollections from our previous tour tell me her room is near the ER side of the hospital and not on the labor and delivery floor. At least I think so, but I'm not sure. I can't focus on hospital geography right now. I am too busy trying to take in everything that is happening and asking a lot of questions. I listen, I watch, then I ask for definitions and clarifications.

In my engineering life, I dwell in a world of black and white, wrong and right. My company is brought in when things go wrong with buildings, and then I figure out what happened and how to fix them. I look, I ask questions, and I probe for answers, both literally and figuratively.

In my mind, there is always a reason, always a cause for the effects, and my job (and my nature) is to figure out the problem so we can work toward solving it. This poor medical team has no idea what kind of high maintenance patient just walked through the door. No, no, not Kylene, she's fairly normal, it's me, Sir Asks-A-Lot, who you should be worried about.

Kylene settles into her patient bed and the team starts observing her vital signs as well as the heartbeats of the babies. Decelerations on Baby Boy seem under control, but now a new wave of concern is cresting. Kylene is starting to have contractions. They seem to be Braxton-Hicks, otherwise known as the false alarm variety of contractions, but they don't seem to be stopping, which raises anxiety for the medical team, for Kylene, and for me. The team believes she is in labor, and I suspect they are silently beginning to prepare for delivery.

On a high level, all this activity is much too early. The babies are in the two-pound range, maybe a little more, but certainly too small to be evicted from their current home. This reality galvanizes all focus and efforts into keeping the babies safely inside for as long as possible.

Now to the details, which are critical to me, the root cause of the excitement. Baby Boy is causing trouble and Kylene's body is receiving signals, or sending them, or both, and the messages are causing the conspiring babies to start planning an early escape. We need to keep an eye on the babies' respective statuses, while also trying to get Kylene's body to relax. Dr. Franco calmly assesses all the factors and prescribes a plan with some intervening medicines. As that is prepared in the background, Kylene insists to me that she can control the contractions.

"These aren't real, it's the position I'm in. If they would just let me adjust the bed back a little and not put me in a crunch, I think it will stop."

I believe her. Or at least I believe that she believes it. We try to convey her theory to the nurses, but we are just background noise in their focused execution of a plan.

"You're in labor, honey," quips a nurse with a tone of condescension.

"I'm telling you, I'm not. It's the position. Let me move the bed and the contractions will stop," she reiterates. Still there is some reason they want her to stay put. Maybe it's the monitoring belts, or maybe it is just the normal setup, but whatever it is, her requests are met with resistance. Not from a place of ignorance, I'm sure, but from experience. With enough insistence from both of us, in a team attack we finally convince someone to let us just try to change her position and see what happens.

They finally yield, so we move the bed according to Kylene's specifications. Within moments, her muscles relax, and the contractions stop. Her instincts were exactly right. Now, instead of pouring gas on the fire of this situation, her body can help extinguish it, lending calm to everyone in the room, particularly to the babies inside. Mama knows best.

With that one big problem abated, at least for now, we reach a much more relaxed state and return focus to the babies and what we can do to help them long-term. After I ask a barrage of questions, we learn the prescribed medicine has nothing to do with delaying the delivery. It doesn't do that at all. It's a steroid. We want them to develop their ability to breathe, ahead of the normal schedule. This is a jump start, so to speak, so that if they do come out early, they can breathe. Right, that seems kind of important.

There is a lot more medical detail which I get from my many questions and further research on my laptop, but the piece that stands out to me is the word "surfactant." That's one I don't know. Evidently, early in lung development, before air is in them, the inside surfaces of the lungs are kind of sticky. If the lungs are deployed ahead of schedule, the sticky surfaces can remain stuck together, so it's harder to pull them apart, which makes it harder to breathe. Surfactant is a surface protein that makes things more slippery, like soap, reducing the stickiness and allowing the babies to breathe easier. The steroid introduces the slippery. I learned something new today.

We also learn that administering the steroid this isn't an instant process and that there will be at least two doses. Translation: Kylene is spending the night. Correction, *we* are spending the night. The contractions have ceased, the heart decelerations have stopped, and now we are just waiting for the steroids to get in there and turn those babies into superhuman little breathers. Spending the night doesn't seem so bad, especially since a few hours ago, we thought they might be born today.

Kylene is exhausted, so even though she is uncomfortable, and sleep usually eludes her these days, she drifts off to sleep almost as soon as the lights are extinguished. That leaves me to fend for myself. My suggestion that the nurses let me use another patient bed is summarily rejected, so I settle into the chair in Kylene's room. Granted it does fold out flat and in theory provides adequate support, for someone 5 foot 8 inches or smaller. I'm much larger than that so I hang off every edge of the surface, but at least I'm laying down. I'm not leaving, so this will have to do.

The night isn't great. There are constant interruptions by dutiful nurses who check Kylene's vitals and the babies' heart monitors. They are doing their jobs, but disruptions every fifteen minutes make for restless sleep for an anxious husband. Aside from the check-ins, though, the night is uneventful. Contractions remain at bay and both the babies' heartbeats are consistent. Crisis averted.

Our relief is palpable, but in the morning we learn Kylene isn't going to be discharged today. She has to spend another night here to receive the second steroid dose and another night of monitoring. We're disappointed. We really want to go home, and the extended stay is not what we expected, but the relief of the babies being okay overrides the frustration, so we can deal with being here one more night. I go home to sleep, eat, and take a shower. When I return, Kylene is still doing well. We endure another uneventful day and night and then finally I am allowed to take her back home.

Bad Rest

After all the hospital excitement we settle back into the bed rest routine but take it up to another level of seriousness. I'm paranoid now. I don't want her walking much or doing much of anything at all. Normally, she isn't one to do nothing all day, but she tries to follow the rules. Her work has been exceptionally gracious and gave her the time off without much fuss proving they truly want the best for her and the babies. So now we wait and hope the babies will cook in the oven for as long as possible.

The idea of bed rest sounds amazing, doesn't it? There are mornings when I want to stay in bed, nestled in the blankets, even if I sleep just another hour, or maybe all day. Imagine having that indulgence be mandatory and doctor prescribed. It seems downright luxurious, what anyone would wish for, but it's really not that great.

There is one main problem: Kylene is not comfortable. Sometimes she toils in generic discomfort, and at other times there are acute surges of pain that leave her gasping for breath. Whether it's nausea, cramping muscles, a headache, heartburn, swollen feet, or some diabolical combination of several ailments, she is seemingly always, and forever, uncomfortable. She tries to relieve the issues, or avoid conditions that inflame them, but the maladies descend regardless of whether she is standing, or sitting, or laying down. She never feels relaxed, and since she can't move to a position that is relaxing, it makes her all the more restless.

There's the rub: Bed rest, no matter how glorious it may seem, isn't very restful at all. To make things worse, she's not only uncomfortable, but it seems she's often thinking about just how uncomfortable she is, which hastens her into a downward spiral of misery. In the rare event that she finds a way to exhale and settle into a tolerable position for even a moment, she'll soon have to get up and go to the bathroom yet another time because there are two little people taking turns bouncing on her bladder. When she returns from the umpteenth bathroom visit, the entire cycle of discomfort resumes. Bed rest is a sentencing to endless hours of conscious misery.

All the discomfort and sacrifice pay off, though, as one week, and then another, passes with the babies still safely inside and growing steadily. It's working, but in the process, she inflicts a lot of pressure on herself. Kylene's singular focus is making it another day, another week, another month. I'm worried too, but I don't think of it every waking moment. She does.

It's painfully ironic really, as Kylene sacrifices herself to make and maintain the absolute most hospitable environment for these two tiny babies, they make things most inhospitable for her. Ungrateful, inconsiderate, little villains, these two. Always causing trouble.

Spanglish

We have eclipsed thirty weeks and are hoping to go much further. On a Monday afternoon, we head to the doctor for another weekly checkup. After the ER trip and the overnight stay, each checkup is a little more nerve-wracking than last. Today, I'm worried about how the twins are faring and particularly how Baby Boy is doing since he is the one who was showing some trouble before. Then again, Kylene has been laying low and doing well, so I remain optimistic. Well, optimistically worried.

We enter the office and breeze through the process like wily veterans—we have now been here so many times that everyone knows us. In the exam room we run through the gamut of external and internal checks with the doctor and then head to the ultrasound room where we watch and listen to heartbeats and just generally check in on the crew. There isn't much movement anymore, not because they've become inactive, but because there is simply less room to move around. It is tight quarters in there and the discomfort is extending to the whole party. Despite the shrinking accommodations, Kylene's body remains calm, the babies are still growing, and they seem to be doing well. The doctor assures us that everything is going fine, Kylene is doing great, and we should just keep doing more of the same.

Good news for today. I'll take it.

I ask the doctor about a work trip I need to take, one last overnight visit to Indianapolis to inspect the production progress at a steel fabrication plant. Since everything is going well, it makes sense to squeeze it in now before it's too late. Dr. Bateman gives the green light, so I schedule the site visit with my client and the fabrication plant. I'll go down tomorrow night, on Tuesday, and make the inspection early Wednesday morning in order to be back home midday Wednesday. Just one last trip and then I don't have to do anything else out of town until after the babies are born.

When I wake up Tuesday morning, I check in with Kylene and she still seems fine. I shower and pack and head to work, expecting to drive down to Indy in the afternoon. On the road, I call Kylene's sister Katie, who lives in our area, to make sure she is around tonight when I'm gone. Just in case. I also call our good friend Tony. He and his wife Stephanie have been some of our closest friends the last few years. Tony has an office close to our house and is an all-around good guy who would do anything for his friends. I call him as a backup to my primary backup in Katie. If Kylene needs something I confirm that she could also call them and between him and Steph, they would find a way to help. Satisfied I have all of my contingencies in place, I finish a morning of work in the office and then make the drive to my hotel. My plan is to visit the steel plant by around 6:00 am, complete the inventory and inspection, and head home. The weather is fine, the roads are clear, and the plant supervisor confirms he's planning on it as well.

I reach my hotel, grab some dinner to eat in my room, and plan for an early night and a very early alarm. I check in with Kylene and she's doing okay. She informs me that Tony had called and insisted on bringing her a Frosty from Wendys. Despite her protestations, he brought it anyway and she was enjoying a moment of rich, creamy indulgence amidst her near constant misery. I'm glad she's enjoying it and thankful that Tony came through, even though he wasn't called upon. Everything is going as planned.

After dinner, I make the mistake of turning on the TV and fall victim to my propensity to watch for too long. There is a basketball game that I casually watch for a few hours and after that finishes instead of turning the TV off, I flip around on the channels and find a movie I've not yet seen: *Spanglish*, an Adam Sandler film where he debuts his abilities to tackle drama instead of comedy.

I decide to check it out, just for a few minutes. Many minutes later, I realize Sandler is pretty good at this genre, that I like the movie, and I'm drawn in. I fall into the same trap all too often. Once I start a film, I like to finish it, even if I have seen it before. With this movie being a new one, I want to see the end. When it finally wraps up, I realize it's after 1:00 am. I have to be up in a few hours to make the 6:00 a.m. inspection appointment. What a dumb decision. I don't know why I did that. Stupid Sandler and his deceptively engrossing film. I'll pay the price tomorrow.

The Call

My alarm sounds at 5 am, waking me from a short bout of sleep—less than four hours. Watching that movie was indeed a big mistake.

Why did I do that? Dumb.

I push through the cobwebs in my mind and run through the motions of showering, inserting my contact lenses, brushing my teeth, getting dressed, and packing my suitcase, albeit in a zombie-like trance. Hotel breakfast service doesn't start until 6:00 am, and since I'm supposed to be on site by that time, I forgo eating and decide to just head straight to the steel production facility. I certainly don't intend to be late, and I know they are waiting for me. There will be plenty of time to grab some food later.

The inspection goes smoothly. I relay a few observations and corrections to the production manager, exchange pleasantries for a while, and then head back out to my truck.

It's after 9:00 am, so I feel like it's safe to call Kylene and check in without fear of waking her. I suspect she is up by now anyway. She answers quickly, and immediately I can sense that things are not good.

"I didn't sleep all night," she begins.

Funny, I didn't either. Did you stay up too late watching a movie? I decide not to offer that comment out loud.

Her opening revelation isn't that surprising or alarming since she's been uncomfortable for weeks, if not months, and never sleeps well.

She continues, "I have terrible pain in my back that won't go away no matter what position I move into. I called the doctor this morning and they said we should go to the hospital. Katie is on her way to pick me up."

Now she has my full attention. I'm actually quite concerned, especially after our scare two weeks ago. I'm expecting a similar, frenzied trip to the hospital, but I'm half of Indiana and a third of Michigan away. I don't want her to have to do all that again without me there. I try to keep my voice calm and reassure her.

"Ok, well, I'll meet you at the hospital. I'm already done with the inspection and can head back now. It's four or five hours from here. I'll get there as soon as I can."

The One

Before I met Kylene painful endings to a few teenage romances had levied heavy tolls on my heart. I didn't understand the valuable life lessons then, and the breakups inflicted painful scars and left damaging residues in the moment.

The second such ending happened early in my senior year of high school. Though I wasn't a perfect boyfriend, I was steadfastly loyal and committed in relationships, so when the ending happened, I took it hard. Maybe harder than I should have. I remember quietly weeping in our family bathroom over the despair of a seventeen-year-old broken heart. My mom heard me and came in to console me. She didn't say much but I remember she commented,

"You just love so deeply."

She didn't mean it as a criticism or a mandate to change, but soon after that night I resigned myself to toughen up yet again. Despite my previously decreed rules of intentional emotional suppression, I was still weak, and I could be better. That really meant closing up further, caring less (or appearing so), and protecting myself even more.

It was settled, my mind was more focused, my heart was fully guarded, and any remaining nonsensical trappings of outward emotions I had let leak out since junior high were gathered up and cast deep into the subterranean caverns of my psyche. I promised myself two things: First, I wasn't going to cry again, not *ever*, because that was stupid, and pathetic, and nothing was worth crying about. Second, the "L" word was off the table, indefinitely. There was no way I was ever telling another girl that I love her again.

I was serious with my pronouncements but looking back now, I'm convinced God watched all these personal edicts with great amusement, perhaps even lovingly smirking at my fastidious resolve. He had other plans. I met Kylene a week later.

My wounds were still fresh and with my new self-limiting proclamations, I was in a weird place. I think if we had started something right then, I would have messed it up, because, frankly, *I* was a little messed up. I was sure that I liked her, and I knew she was special, but I needed to wait.

So, we were friends first, really good friends, and there was a spark. Something real and palpable. I had lots of friends and a lot of them were girls, but none were like her. She was the only one who made me feel this way, but we didn't date. Not officially, not even unofficially. We both said we were just friends, but my heart said otherwise.

The truth is I've been in love with Kylene since then, since way before we started dating. She will dispute the nuances of the timeline, but I know what I know. It just took me a while to heal and get myself straightened out. Once I did, I had turned eighteen and most of my senior year had gone by. After months of spending countless hours on the phone, and many weekend nights hanging out, and just generally being around each other as much as possible, it was time to stop waiting. It was time to go.

Finally, one April afternoon after school, I went straight to find Kylene at her job downtown at The Paper Place. I walked in and after a little small talk, I asked her to prom, somewhat out of the blue, right there in the store. I don't know if she was expecting it, but I was nervous, my heart pounding with the thrill of asking. When she accepted, the excitement turned to relief, and then morphed again into pure elation. I had never felt so affirmed in a decision. I left and went out to Coast Guard Park where I was meeting a bunch of my friends for a pickup game of basketball. I was in such a good mood, boiling over with joy and confidence. I played the game of my life, hitting every shot, connecting on every pass. It felt so right. Everything felt right.

That first step opened the door for more and soon after, we had our first kiss. It was spontaneous, but overdue, and my head started to comprehend what my heart had known for a long time. I realized I was falling hard for Kylene, and fast. Weeks later, I picked her up on prom night, and it was all over for me. I remember the way she looked and the dress she wore. It was silver and sparkly. All night, I was so happy to be with her, and all I saw was her. She had been worth waiting for.

After a wonderful summer of dating, as August faded, I was on the threshold of leaving for college while she still had a year of high school, and we were forced to discuss what we were going to do with our relationship. We sat at the beach and talked, and I mentioned I wanted to try the long-distance option and see how it went. Relief washed over me when she confirmed she wanted to stay together, and I held her that much more tightly as we gazed at the stars on one of the clearest nights of my life. As we sat there with hopes for the future, we saw not one, but dozens of shooting stars, one after another. It was as if God orchestrated the universe to shower us with signs of confirmation.

I distinctly recall her first visit to Ann Arbor when I was away at college. She was wearing a white shirt and a light white sweater and after she parked illegally in the bus lane behind my dorm she got out of the car and ran to me. She jumped into my arms, and I lifted her off the ground in an embrace. We had survived the first month of long-distance dating. I had waited so long to see her, and hold her and finally, after all that time, it was so great to feel like everything was okay. We lasted the year and then she opted to attend the same college, giving us convenient proximity. We led our own lives, had our own friend groups and experiences, but we saw each other a lot and stayed together throughout.

Five years after I started, college was done for me, we were engaged, and I began my first year living and working in Chicago. I was there alone, having finished graduate school and started my career, while she stayed behind to finish her own graduate degree program. Every other week or so, one of us would make the journey from Chicago to Ann Arbor, or vice versa, to see each other. It was usually me going. She was still in school with homework, and I wasn't, so I would make the trip every week or two. It was a mind-numbing, endless trek along Interstate 94, one of the least interesting corridors through an otherwise beautiful state. I would wait all week, try to get out of work early, and then I'd drive as fast as I could with as few stops as possible. I despised that drive and that road, and all the trucks along the highway, but I made the trip so many times because I desperately needed to get to Kylene. That road led to her, and that was always more than worth the trip.

I remember my frayed nerves as I stood waiting at the end of the church aisle on our wedding day, my heart celebrating in relief when the doors finally opened and she was actually standing there, simply stunning. I remember the look on her face and the light in her eyes, thinking how I was so lucky, but knowing how she was the one for me.

Our early married years in Chicago saw us both working lots of hours and traveling frequently, often going a full week or more without seeing each other. I missed her and always anxiously waited for her to get home or impatiently waited in airports so I could get home to her. It seemed like an endless cycle; always waiting and hurrying to get to her.

When we decided to leave Chicago and move back to West Michigan, the timing of our job transitions dictated that I moved first, and we were separated again for a month. This time, she would travel to me, and we would spend the weekends searching for a house. It was exciting, but stressful, as we planted seeds for the rest of our lives in short forty-eight-hour increments, all while living apart for the weekdays in between. During the week, I was staying alone in my aunt and uncle's unoccupied condo, watching the Olympics every night by myself. The condo was great, and things were exciting as I started a new job and was learning my way around a new city, but it was hollow. Something was missing. *She* was missing. Once again, I was waiting for her, and I couldn't really start this next chapter of life until she was with me.

Over the last several months since the pregnancy began, our excitement has been growing in parallel with her rapidly expanding belly, but once again, I find myself waiting. Waiting for fatherhood. Waiting for the babies to arrive. Waiting for this big change. And all the while, as I wait, things are already beginning to change. The feeling of "us" that we have had since prom night is slowly being infiltrated by the nebulous "them" — the babies. Even though we are waiting for them, in some ways they are already here. First it was just in concept, but soon they began to take up physical space. Our family is literally doubling in size, and my allegiances and responsibilities are broadening. The babies are already the focus of everything we do. They dominate all our conversations, our dreams, our worries, our preparations, our financial savings and spendings, and even our physical bodies. They are so loved and considered in every thought, every movement, and every decision. They already occupy the majority of our collective consciousness.

The colossal shift in priorities has affected both of us, though in somewhat different ways. In Kylene's mind, whether she sees it or not, the babies have elevated to become her sole concern, to the extent that she disregards herself and her own needs in order to meet theirs. Meanwhile, even though concern for the twins occupies much of my mind as well, they haven't displaced her.

No one can do that. She remains at the absolute center of my world and of my worries, because even with the babies in the mix, she is still the one, my only one. And my one is in crisis with our babies, and I have never been more impatient to close the distance between us. I think about all the time we spent apart when I first started school, when I moved to Chicago, and when I first moved back to Michigan. All of that time we spent waiting for each other, but none of it felt like this.

The waiting needs to end, and now, more than ever before, I need to go to her.

Part V - Arrivals

92

Indianapolis Speedway

There are loosely documented stories from various segments of recorded history highlighting moments in which people respond to crises in ways that seem impossible. Tales of legend, featuring miraculous endeavors that grow in their embellishment the more times the stories are shared. In most such stories, temporary superhuman abilities are somehow acquired and facilitate inexplicable feats — lifting a car, swimming for hours in stormy waters, repeatedly running into a burning building, or enduring weeks without food or water — things everyone wants to hear about, stories that are told over and over, and people might even choose to write a book about. Touché.

At this moment, as I hang up the phone and my current crisis looms, I don't receive any miraculous giftings. No bestowed superpowers, no visionary enlightenment, no solution to my evolving dilemma. Instead, I am graced with one singular focus.

Drive.

I'm deep in the heart of an industrial center on the east side of Indianapolis, two hundred and ninety miles away from my destination. I start the engine in the brisk November morning air and quickly maneuver the truck out of the poorly maintained asphalt parking lot, down the local access street, turn west down 30th street, north for about a mile and then find my way on to I-465 which encircles all of greater downtown Indy. I stay northbound on I-465 until I can exit on to I-69 toward Fort Wayne.

Normally, the drive to or from the shop takes me four to five hours, depending on traffic and the time of day. But today, I want to move faster. I need to move faster. As I race down the highway, I contemplate just how fast I can go, how closely I can tiptoe toward the edge of reason, all the while weighing the potential pitfalls of a complete disregard for sanity. Arrested for reckless driving and evading police? Those seem like things I'd like to avoid. Careening off the freeway into a bridge abutment culminating in a pile of flaming wreckage? I'd like to skip that scene as well. Somehow, leaving my unborn children without a father seems to defeat the purpose of my rushing.

My body is tense, my head and heart are pounding, and I desperately want to get there. I settle on a speed range and an upper threshold for which I'll simply plead the fifth. It isn't a triple digit number, but there are strategic flirtations with such speeds on a few occasions. Even as I mentally rehearse my speech for the state trooper that will inevitably record my speed and pull me over, I press my foot down on the accelerator just a bit more, set the cruise control, and rocket through the miles of recently harvested Indiana corn fields.

I have plenty of fuel, I don't need to eat, and if I have to go, well, I'm just going to hold it. Yes, the whole way.

There is no stopping, there is not even any braking. Lane position changes and minor cruise control adjustments is all I allow as I maneuver in and out of motorists operating at various reasonable speeds. My truck is moving faster than any of the other cars, and the endlessly straight segments of freeway stream past in a blur.

My vision is a tunnel, my eyes laser-focused on the road looking for potential obstacles ahead. My hands grip and manipulate the wheel with the deft precision of a Formula car driver. My calm, steady movements belie my anxiety and impatience. Blessed with light traffic, no sign of cops, and moderate weather for the last day in November, the minutes and miles evaporate behind me as I will myself forward.

Suddenly, I'm rounding into the S-curve in downtown Grand Rapids. I've made it here unscathed and without being apprehended by the authorities. Though unofficial, I'm quite certain that records have fallen, that I hold a new land-speed record—not in the salt flats of Utah, but right here in western Michigan. That or I've found an elusive wormhole somewhere near the state border. Either way, this is the miracle I needed.

Just after 1:00 pm, I exit off from Michigan Street into the hospital parking structure. Having been here for at least two recent trips, I know my way quite well.

Need to See

I find the check-in desk and am directed back to the room where Kylene and the babies are being monitored. I knock and enter to find Kylene in the bed, Katie by her side and the doctor reviewing a clipboard. Two heart monitors are connected to Kylene's belly, and everyone seems focused on the output screens. Dr. Bateman glances up long enough to see me walk in.

"Good, you're here." Only her tone isn't a message of welcome. It suggests my arrival marked the finalization of something. They have been waiting for me.

Relief washes over Kylene, knowing now that I am not going to miss anything important. But tension still fills the air, and serious decisions are looming. My eyes scan the room imploringly, searching for someone to catch me up. Between Kylene and Doctor Bateman I get a quick recap: He is experiencing decels again.

We still just say "he" and we both know what that means. We know his name but haven't shared it with anyone; in fact, we almost never speak their names in private either. It is as if we believe there might be some large government or family-supported eavesdropping campaign occurring in our living room. Someone has bugged our house, and they are listening for us to trip up and spill the names, so we rarely let down our guard.

We don't say them out loud, but we know the names and love them. I've already cut out twenty-four-inch-tall capital letter initials for each of them from a sheet of MDF plywood. A big letter R and a big letter E. We refer to them as "the letters" since the initials remain shrouded in secrecy as well. I painted the letters white, together we added pink and blue custom accents by hand, and then I hung them in the nursery above their respective cribs. The initials are up; the names are set.

Anyway, spoiler alert, the R is for him, and he is not doing well. Decels are those decelerations again — temporary reductions in his heart rate. These periodic signs of irregularity are what led to our last hospital visit and now the conditions seem worse. Baby Boy is in distress, and Dr Bateman is concerned it may only decline further. Only minutes have passed since I walked in the door, but she concludes,

"We need to take the babies out. Today. I'm going to go prep for surgery."

With that mercilessly heavy statement, the air is sucked out of the room, or at least out of my lungs. The doctor exits, the door closes, and the nursing staff begin a hurried, practiced, sequence of preparations.

Conceptually, I understood the reasoning. He is in distress, it is risky to wait, and the doctor thinks the best chance is to get them out and make sure they're safe.

But taking them out now is risky too. They need to cook in the oven a lot longer. It's too early for them. They are nine weeks too early. What is happening?

The nurses are moving quickly around the room, expertly executing the plan, but my mind can't catch up. I'm still standing here, wondering how everything changed so fast. It feels like everything is moving forward but I'm stuck in neutral, battling to regain control.

Preparing for surgery also means they need to prep Kylene. She needs to change clothes, get transferred into the operating room, and get her spinal tap going. That all makes sense as well, but it means she's leaving too. The nurses explain where she's headed and begin to usher me out the door so they can get her ready.

"Then we'll all reconvene in the O.R. Ready then? Okay, let's go."

Only I'm not ready. I'm not ready at all.

"I need to see the doctor," I say to the nearest nurse I can find.

"She's preparing for surgery, she's not available right now."

"I need to talk to her." I'm insistent.

"What are your questions? I can go talk to Dr. Bateman and get them answered for you."

Still, I persist and again repeat my demand to see the doctor.

I'm sure everyone says the same thing. Everyone needs to see the doctor, even when the nurses are more than capable. Everyone has questions. But they don't understand that I'm not everyone and that my situation is different. This is my life, my entire existence, hanging in the balance, precariously dangling over a gorge of uncertainty. My wife, my daughter, and my son—who you just determined is already in trouble—all their lives are suddenly at risk. Everything is at risk. My everything.

I need to talk to the doctor. Not just any doctor, not whoever happens to be on call tonight. Our doctor. She has been at nearly every appointment with us. She was at the ultrasound appointments. She always talked *with* us and not *at* us. She knows both of our names. Every time I see her, she greets me with an elaborate bro-style handshake or first bump, always initiated by her. She makes me feel important and always includes me in every discussion. She was the one who suspected multiples at that fateful appointment so many months ago, she was with us to encourage and reassure us along the way, and she calmly explained everything when the two twenty-somethings morphed from excited first-time expectant parents into petrified kids expecting twins. She catapulted our care into the high-risk category. More appointments, more ultrasounds, more everything and at her urging, we couldn't see her PA or NP. All appointments were with her. She altered her schedule to see us. She demanded the bed rest and had been preparing for this moment for the last many months. I need to talk to the doctor. I need to talk to *our* doctor.

I don't know if I am particularly eloquent or otherwise compelling, but somehow, they can tell I am serious, or determined, or terrified, or most likely, all of the above.

"I just need to talk to the doctor before we start," I plead.

The nurses acquiesce.

"We'll find her."

Within a few minutes, Dr Bateman comes back. Kylene is still being prepared elsewhere, so it's just me in the room. She enters with speed, moving with clear purpose, and exhibits just the slightest touch of irritation. Irritation with me. She has important things to do. Nevertheless, she has come back. As she steps through the door, I realize she's wearing scrubs. Common attire within a hospital no doubt, but I've never seen her in scrubs before. All of our previous meetings took place in her OB/GYN office during planned appointments. She was always dressed nicely and whatever outfit she wore was topped with her white doctor coat festooned with her name in black block print. Seeing her in the scrubs is a noticeable change. I am again reminded of the reality that serious things are about to happen.

She gets right to the point. "What's up? What do you need?"

"I need to know what's about to happen. I mean, what's actually going to happen in there?"

"Okay, sure. He is in distress, so we are going to do an emergency C-section. We will cut the tummy, quickly pull out Baby Girl because she's first in line, so that we can get to Baby Boy. Then we'll get him out.

"You will see each of them briefly, but you won't get to hold them, you won't be cutting the cords, none of that. There will be a lot of people in there, a whole team of doctors and nurses for each baby. Once they are stabilized, they will be taken out of the room and up to the NICU. Then I will stitch Kylene back up and she'll go to the recovery floor. Do you understand?"

"Yes. Thank you. That's helpful. I just needed to know what to expect."

"Let's go get your babies," she says, and she leaves again in a hurry.

Alone again. Alone with my thoughts and a lot of new information. With stress mounting and worry escalating, I put on the provided scrubs and settle into a holding pattern. Waiting. I had asked the doctor what would happen, and she told me, plain and simple, but now everything is different. The birth plan and those classes we took—obsolete. The challenges of labor, the timing between contractions, wrestling with the decision of when we should go to the hospital. How far is she dilated, how far apart are the contractions—irrelevant.

The sequence of steps, the waiting, the strategy, the pushing, and the breathing. Ah, yes, the breathing. Lest my reprimand for misdirected exhalation be repeated or worse, I had revised and perfected my breathing and coaching plan. The novel brilliance of my new strategy would be that of legends. I was going to turn my head away, far away, from my wife. A freestyle swimmer gliding through the water, deftly turning for a gulp of air while maintaining the rhythm and flow of his mission. I would do the most amazing breath coaching while managing to never bother her with even the slightest breeze announcing my existence. I had it all worked out, but now that solution has been smothered as well. No need for breathing. No pushing. No storybook moment of the first time holding my babies, no traditional dad cutting of the cord. Gone. That is all gone. Not happening. At least not how I had planned and envisioned it in my mind.

It is disappointing, but only for a fleeting moment. I don't mourn it for long, I just needed to know, and now that I do, the new reality lands with finality. At least there is a plan. It isn't our plan, but this is how it is going to be. Now I know, and so I wait.

A nurse arrives to tell me that they're ready. She leads me across the hall and directs me to a set of doors that are apparently the operating room.

Wait, what? It's right here?

I had imagined someplace further away. Somewhere in the building of course, but not one room away. It seems ill-fitting, almost wrong. Where is the long, stark corridor that I must traverse? The setting for some cinematic moment in which I steel myself and build my resolve for the life-altering challenge ahead. There's no climactic hallway, no dramatic lighting, not even a soundtrack-worthy song. The door is right there just waiting for me. I was sort of counting on that longer hallway, I needed the runway, because I'm not ready and I fear what's on the other side of those doors.

"And over here is the room you'll enter when one or both of your twins' lives are in danger and they're nine weeks early and your wife has to have an emergency Cesarean section surgery and your life comes to a screeching halt while simultaneous spinning out of control and you're worried you'll lose everything you care about…"

This room had not been on the tour.

City Slickers

There is a scene in the 1991 film *City Slickers* that echoes in my memory. In the comedy turned western, three friends, played by Billy Crystal, Daniel Stern, and Bruno Kirby, embark on a cattle drive adventure. I don't want to spoil it for you, but let's be honest, the movie has been out for over thirty years, so you've had your chance to see it by now.

Here's the basic premise: Mitch (Crystal) is feeling unfulfilled in life, languishing in a pointless job, and staring into the abyss of his inevitable aging. As indifference festers, his unhappiness grows and it begins to impact his family life leading his wife to make a soft, but harrowing, ultimatum. The friends take the trip to help him get away and to obey his wife's directive of coming back renewed and only after he is able to "find his smile." Colorful characters and comical sequences abound as the three middle-aged men, born and raised in the paved enclosures of New York City, mount horses, rope cattle, and sleep under the stars. You should really watch it; it mostly stands the test of time.

In the middle of the film, during a long, slow day of riding, the friends find themselves deep in meaningful conversation and wade into playing a game of sorts, where each must reveal the best day and worst day of their lives. Mitch celebrates his first Yankees game with his dad and laments a day his wife had a breast cancer scare. Phil (Stern) reflects on the happiness of his wedding day and comically mourns his worst day as every day of marriage since. After insistent urging to participate, Ed (Kirby) reluctantly shares his best day from a situation when he was fourteen. It was the day he stood up to his abusive father, vowed he would take care of his mother and sister, and suggested his dad leave. His dad obliged, left that day, and he never saw him again.

Incredulous, Phil challenges Ed's choice,

"…That's your best day? What's your worst day?"

A wounded expression on his face, Ed responds, "Same day," before he rides off by himself.

Pause the movie. This moment is my entry point into the most important role and responsibility of my life—being a dad. It's the best day of my life.

But I am crippled with fear, worry and helplessness. Will my babies have a normal life? Will my babies even live? Will my wife survive? It's the worst day of my life.

Same day.

Useless

With the weight of the world pressing down, threatening to crush my shoulders and telescope my spine, I walk through the double doors and into the rest of my life.

I'm surprised at how large the room is and by the number of people already assembled. Everyone is in position. It feels as if I'm the last straggler to arrive for a surprise party, but I'm not the guest of honor, far from it. I am the least significant person in the room. They all tolerate my presence, but I am completely unnecessary. Just another bumbling numbskull soon-to-be-dad who doesn't know what's going on. Useless.

There is the sound of indistinct chatter from a swarm of doctors and nurses to my right. Each is clad in all the typical paraphernalia — masks, hats, scrubs, and gloves — and they are busy preparing sterile instruments and two separate receiving stations. In the center of the room is a large table with lights and other expensive-looking equipment mounted overhead.

Kylene is lying on her back on the table with a blue surgery drape positioned just below her chest. Her belly and much of her lower half are exposed. Dr Bateman stands on the far side of the table, to Kylene's right, preparing her instruments and checking some of the monitors. At least I think she's standing, it's actually hard to tell. She is a petite woman; I would guess no more than 5 ft-2 inches. At 6 ft-1 in, I'm not massively tall by the standards of my Dutch heritage, but I tower over her diminutive frame. Still, she commands the room, looming large with her full personality, a force to be reckoned with. Though small in stature, she is someone I trust and respect. Amidst the noise, the whirlwind of emotions, the worry, and all the uncertainty, I realize in that moment just how glad I am that it's her in here with us today. There is no one else on earth I want with us in this room. Having her familiar face, our advocate, our team, means absolutely everything right now. And on this day, it's the one thing that has gone right.

At the head of the table, directly behind Kylene, is the anesthesiologist. He tells me his name which I immediately forget. He is perched on a stool as he manipulates his equipment, constantly adjusting the formula of the chemical cocktail coursing through Kylene's body via a spinal block. This procedure introduces the chemicals directly into the cerebrospinal fluid. Into her spine.

He makes sure the spinal is effective by touching her legs and torso.

"Can you feel that? How about that? How about now?" I'm watching and listening, and frankly, I'm very interested.

As Kylene answers, he makes the adjustments and eventually she says she can't feel anything below the drape. Perfect. Now I'm worried about her being paralyzed.

Is this process really our present level of sophistication?

Despite my misgivings, the guy is kind, calm and the only person really talking to us. He's also the only medical person who is, shall we say, north of the equator. Everyone else is south of the separating drape making final preparations. Then, all of a sudden, it's go time.

Blood Drive

I'm a little scared, filled with anticipation, excited for the amazing things about to happen, but fearing for the worst. Oddly, the only thing I'm not worried about is handling the surgery, I know for certain I'll be fine with that part.

I know because I've always been good with blood. I've been plagued with bloody noses since I was a little kid. Dry membranes, a stiff breeze, the quiver of a dragonfly's back leg, it seemed anything could trigger a nosebleed for me. My first memories of nosebleeds were when they would come at night - I would make a mess of my bed sheets and pajamas. It happened so much, Mom eventually taught me how to soak things in cold water and how to clean up after myself. They happened at school, at church, seemingly everywhere. They were indiscriminate and often inconvenient, but I was prepared, comfortable, and had a controlled response, even when adults around me were freaking out. I knew the taste (Gross, right? Well, I do), and I could sense one coming before it arrived. I knew how to deal with it, and it was just part of my life. No big deal.

My blood exposure résumé ramped up further in high school when I was on Student Senate and in charge of our school blood drive. This job meant creating and peddling all the posters, reminding classmates they can save up to four lives per donation, sacrificing many lunch periods staffing the signup table, and the final big day in the gym when all the chairs were wheeled in, the nurses set up at their stations, and the donations actually happened. Wait here, now sit here, just a pinch, do you feel okay, have a cookie, wait fifteen minutes, thanks for coming. Repeat.

Throughout the years, most student donors did well, but I witnessed a wide spectrum of other responses. Fainting, fear of needles, lightheadedness, nausea. Stuff happened. Whether it was a small teenage girl barely meeting the minimum donation weight requirements or the largest lineman from the football team, I never could quite predict who would be scared, who would cry, or who would pass out. If I were to handicap it now, my money is on one of the big guys. Big trees fall hard. What I do know is I saw blood; I saw lots of blood. I watched it come down the hose and fill the bags. I transported the bags around on carts from the stations to the refrigeration areas. I saw all the blood, I witnessed all the personal issues, for hours on end, and none of it bothered me at all. Naturally, I concluded that I must have been tougher than those football players who were fainting.

In my twenties, I realized that amidst all the blood drive fanfare in high school, I had never actually donated. Perhaps my smug disposition toward those football players had been premature. It was time to find out.

I went in to donate and to my delight, it went well. So, I went again. And again. I became a regular. I was helping people, saving up to three lives per pint (the numbers evidently changed since high school. I don't know what happened to that fourth guy). I was giving all the time. I even had the white American Red Cross wallet card with the literal Red Cross emblem in the upper left-hand corner and blue block lettering across the top. Ross Smith, blood type O negative.

Every sixty days or so I'd get the reminder phone call and dutifully head over to the donation center. I considered it a game and made it a competition.

How quickly can I extract the pint this month? Let's see if I can cut 15 seconds off my last time.

I would actually open and close my hand, forming and releasing a tight fist, literally squeezing the blood out. I experimented with different pulsing rhythms and arm placements. I was an expert, the best, but no one else cared. The group of retiree volunteers certainly weren't taking any notice of the feat of excellence being demonstrated in their very midst. It was a feat nevertheless! Victory was on my doorstep. Eight to ten minutes? Please. I could fill that bag in five minutes and twenty three seconds. Give or take.

I digress. Needless to say, the surgery is the least of my worries. I'm good there, I can deal with needles and blood in my sleep.

Welcome to the World

(Day 1 - November 30, 2005)

The receiving teams are ready, and the spinal is dialed in. Dr. Bateman is right of the table and I'm on Kylene's left at the head of the table, next to the anesthesiologist. The nurse smears a generous amount of brown antiseptic on Kylene's belly and lower abdomen, and everything begins. Dr Bateman reaches across the table pulling the scalpel toward herself and creating a low transverse incision. Interested, I watch it happen, flesh separating, and some blood and white fat cells coming out. I don't observe for long and refocus my attention on Kylene who is fully conscious. She doesn't feel it, thankfully. The spinal is doing its job.

I don't choose to watch further as the doctor continues carefully cutting layers to get down to the babies. She asks her team for various instruments, and regularly requests irrigation and suction to clear her field of view. I notice the large, graduated canister collecting everything that comes through the suction pump they keep using. It's pretty big, I would guess its volume is three liters or more. The clear plastic reservoir seemed harmless enough before everything started. It had just been sitting there, sterile, and empty. Now it's active, and it's filling fast. Filling with blood.

"That's a lot of blood," I remark aloud. "Should she be losing that much blood?"

The doctor responds, "Oh, that's mostly water, that's normal."

Uh huh. Right. Like you'd tell me if that wasn't normal.

I had been doing so well, and I had been so confident, but now my head starts swimming a little.

Though she can't feel pain from what's going on in her belly, Kylene can feel movement and we are both surprised at how much motion there is. Beyond the drape, her lower body is moving side to side. The whole table is moving back and forth. Maybe not the table, that's probably secured to the floor, but Kylene is involuntarily wiggling, a lot. I look up to realize the procedure is much more physical than I had expected, both for Kylene the patient, and the team. Dr. Bateman is literally up on the table straddling Kylene and her hands are inside Kylene's body, while other team members are pulling and stretching muscles, physically working to widen the opening to extract the first baby.

More wiggling, pulling, and stretching and then, all of a sudden, she's out.

"Meet your baby girl!" exclaims Dr. Bateman as she holds her up to show us briefly. I stand up to see her, and, already exhibiting classic dad behavior, I am armed with a digital camera. Previous negotiations with Kylene had yielded the compromise that I am allowed to take pictures of the babies, as long as I take care not to photograph too much of the nether regions. (Video, was not on the mother-approved list. I am not even sure the hospital allows that sort of thing anyway.) As I raise the camera, in an instant, two things happen simultaneously. I get the picture and I fall in love.

In the doctor's hands, in front of my eyes is our tiny baby. A life that God ordained, created from me and Kylene, that we've been talking to and about for many months. Our baby girl. I love her. There is no more simple or powerful statement than that. I love her, I am worried about her, and I want to protect her all in the same moment. She is handed off to the first receiving team who initiate a battery of measurements, start clearing her airway, and work feverishly to get her stabilized. The nurse turns to me and asks if we have a name.

The name? No, I can't tell you that. The name is secret.

Nobody knows the names. Privately we know the names, we've been dwelling on that information and keeping it to ourselves. In a world so intent on knowing everything, every decision, every private detail, the names were ours. The letters are on the wall, but no one has seen them. I look at Kylene as if to confirm it's ok to finally say it. Out loud.

"It's Eden." I'm not even sure if I said it or if Kylene said it, but it was finally uttered in public. The secret is out. She is here. Our girl, Eden Smith. Time of birth 2:52 pm.

"We made the right decision, his bag is empty," announces Dr. Bateman with a tone of affirmation. His amniotic sac had been compromised, allowing his amniotic fluid to leak. He was in distress, his heart rate was decelerating, and his growth was slowing, all because his growth compartment wasn't working properly anymore. I am overwhelmed with relief that we hadn't waited. And just after her declaration of justification she holds him up as well.

"Here's your baby boy."

He is here. Our son. The whirlwind of feelings begins all over again. Our little boy, even tinier than his sister, another gift of life from God. My son. The one whose ultrasound profile looks like mine with the same nose and lips, who we've seen clearly sucks his thumb, who has been kicking his mother, and has been getting kicked in the head by his sister. I love him so much. This is my boy, the one who will carry our family name, who will be my buddy. I love him. My son.

As Dr. Bateman holds him up, I stand again and attempt to get a picture, but my focus is off. The baby is blurry and so is everything else. Only it's not the camera, it's me. The swimming feeling in my head has intensified. Dr. Bateman recognizes the look on my face and sees what is coming.

"Ross, sit down," she instructs calmly, but sternly.

"But I want to see him."

The anesthesiologist interjects, "If you go down, we are leaving you on the floor. You are not our concern right now."

They have seen this movie before. The blood, the babies, the worry, the relief, the remaining unknowns. My mental engine is redlining, I'm overwhelmed, and the shadows are closing in. Without moving from his position, the anesthesiologist gently helps me back down to my stool beside him. Meanwhile, our boy is handed to the second receiving team and undergoes the same tests and stabilization routine as his sister. The same nurse asks again if we have a name. I'm dizzy but more confident this time that the secret can be revealed.

"Roman. His name is Roman."

Roman Smith. Time of birth 2:52 pm. The same minute, nearly the same moment.

Both names have now been verbalized. Having been so long awaited, it feels weird but good. Saying the names out loud seems so official, so real, so… permanent. Roman and Eden. Eden and Roman. Welcome to the world.

Another nurse hands me a Styrofoam cup with a lid and straw already inserted.

"Drink this, it's orange juice. The sugar will help," she advises.

I do as I'm told and suck down the sweet nectar of clarity. I manage to maintain consciousness and as I start to get my head back under control, I'm feeling a little embarrassed. Not so tough after all. Instead of coming through for Kylene when things got intense, my first moment as a dad was a major flop. Thankfully, no breathing or coaching or anything remotely resembling useful was necessary for me today. My imaginary knighthood has been revoked. Sir Lancelot is conquered, sitting in the corner, slurping his juice.

Whisked Away

(Day 1- in the NICU)

As I start to regain focus, the medical teams continue working to stabilize the twins while Dr. Bateman starts stitching Kylene back together. Eden stabilizes first and Roman right after, so the teams prepare to move them to the neonatal intensive care unit, commonly referred to as the NICU.

Then, as quickly as they came, the babies are whisked away, out of the room and out of my sight, to a nebulous destination I've heard of, but have never seen. They are leaving, just as the doctor had warned me, and no invitation for me is extended to travel with them. Perhaps this exclusion is due to my general uselessness in this critical moment, or because I could barely stand a few minutes ago. Regardless, the staff reassure me my kids will be safely transported to the NICU where they will be cared for. We can go up and see them any time.

I still don't like it, but I don't really have a choice, and I must trust that these doctors and nurses know what is best. I understand they are medical professionals and see this kind of thing every day; I get that. That doesn't make it any easier to accept. The arrival chapter of my children's lives has concluded and now the survival chapter has begun. I remain on my stool, exhausted and defeated, as I wait to be told what I should do next.

In the midst of the waning excitement a nurse hands me a slip of white paper with handwriting in blue ink. The notations read:

Baby A (Eden)

3 pounds 12 ounces

APGARs 5 and 7

15 ½ inches

Baby B (Roman)

3 pounds, 7 ounces

16 ½ inches

APGARs 5 and 7

The weights are low, so low. The APGAR scores aren't great either (I later learned more about APGARs and realized the scores were a bit concerning). I don't know what they mean and reveal my obliviousness by asking,

"Are these good?"

My only reassurance comes with a response of,

"They're improving."

I don't know anything or know any better in the moment. I'll later learn the 5s aren't good, below average for sure, and at one minute post birth, a score of 5 means all of the five assessment categories averaged a 1 out of 2. Better than zero, I guess, but not the 8 and 9 cumulative score we're aiming for. At five minutes post birth, the second scores are amassed and totaled 7. Closer to normal and an improvement for sure. I'll take it. I'm quickly learning to recognize and celebrate the small victories.

For now, I just know these are their scores and the first record of their existence, so I accept the piece of paper, fold it, and put it in my wallet. I don't know why I did that, why I kept it, but I did.

Part VI - Overload

Insurance

Between crises, shortly after the surgery, I call the director of human resources at my work. I need to make sure insurance is notified or activated or whatever is needed. I'd say today qualifies as a change in family status.

When we found out about the pregnancy, I had called HR to ask a lot of first-time parent questions about coverage and adding a baby to the policy. The director let me blather on about all my concerns and remained patient and helpful. When we later found out about having twins, I called her again with more questions and some panic. Again, she steadied me with her resourcefulness and reassurances.

This time I call from my cell phone in the hospital lobby, pacing circle after circle around an interior water feature, as I tell her what's happening. The twins came way early, we need to get them on the plan, and I am worried about the NICU and all the costs. Will all this specialty care be covered, and if not, what am I supposed to do?

She blesses me with her composure. She tells me congratulations, don't worry about anything, and go take care of your family. She will manage the rest of the paperwork and other notifications. Somewhere in the brief call she reminds me I only have to pay for the base fee at the hospital for each patient.

"It's a two-hundred-dollar flat rate for each patient in that hospital."

"Ok, so four hundred dollars, that's not bad at all."

"No, it's six hundred dollars," She gently corrects.

"Why six?"

"You have three patients. Each of the two babies and your wife."

Three. The stark reality strikes me like a freight train, and I stop pacing, startled for a moment by this realization. I had not been thinking of Kylene as a patient at all. I mean, I knew she was in the hospital, but was thinking about the twins and all the care they would need. I wasn't even thinking about the fact that she just had surgery. Husband fail.

The Third Patient

With Kylene's surgery complete she is being moved upstairs to the fifth floor. It is a general recovery floor because sadly, she doesn't need typical labor and delivery care. She's just a postoperative patient, and the babies won't be with her in the room at all. Until now, I had only thought about c-sections as being a different way to retrieve the babies; in all the excitement, it was lost on me Kylene just had surgery. Major surgery, with a lightning rod poked into her spine, her abdomen slices wide open, and two other people forcibly yanked from within her. Kind of a big day for her, and for me I guess, as pathetic as it seems to even be thinking of myself on a day like today.

I tag along as Kylene is transported to the recovery room, and on the way, she asks to go see the babies. Dr. Bateman insists that she remain in her recovery room at least an hour to ensure she herself is stable. Once in her room, she and I confer to make some parenting decisions. The conversation centers around logistics. Whereas it was easy to transport the family when three of them were in one body (even if on a tandem bicycle), now the twins are out and on a different floor entirely. I can't be both here and there. Kylene's inclination is that I should go up and see the babies and then come back for her in exactly one hour. I'm conflicted. Of course, I want to go to them, but I also don't want to leave her. She is in pain, has a freshly closed incision, is still coming off her spinal tap medicine, and feels just as scared and worried as me. Yet, her maternal instincts are already blazing and she's thinking only of them and not herself.

"I am fine here. Go up and see them."

I realize I was mistaken, and this is not really a conversation at all. It was more of a command, dispatching a newly minted deputy. The directive is loud and clear. I'm leaving.

Blameless

I'm still torn but I leave—out her door, down the hall, and up the elevator to the seventh floor to the NICU. As the elevator doors glide open and I step out for my inaugural visit, I stumble into the lobby not knowing where to go or what to do. A helpful staff person escorts me to the scrub-in room where she teaches me the protocol for NICU visitors. In this room and on this floor, detailed handwashing is serious business and maybe a little foreign to anyone not in the medical field. Remove rings and watches, roll up sleeves and scrub all the way to your elbows. Every trip, every visit, every time. If you leave the area and return, the process starts all over again. Initially, I'll admit, it feels excessive, but I'll soon come to realize how critical it is to keep things here as clean as possible.

Once I've finished the scrubbing, I follow the escort to an intersection in the main hallway. We turn left, north, in the direction of the NICU. The neonatal intensive care unit, the most specialized, most intense care in the hospital for the smallest, most frail of patients. Except for some airlifts and ground transports via ambulance bringing troubled newborns to the facility, these babies have never left the hospital. Like my kids, they have all come straight up here, born directly into crisis and they don't even know it. Some have come to grow and develop, others to correct significant physical issues. Some will be here a few days, some many difficult months, and sadly, some will live the remaining days of their short lives here. Our family journey through this space has just begun, and the outcome is uncertain.

Left at the intersection, down another starkly adorned hallway, past some nursing stations, and left again into the NICU ward. For the second time today, I'm surprised by what I see. I didn't know what to expect, and yet, I didn't expect this. The rectangular room is fairly large, much bigger than a standard one or two patient space. The perimeter features eight to ten stations, each capable of hosting what I can only describe as an incubator, though I'm not certain it's the right term. Perhaps that is a crude or outdated description; after all, these aren't baby chickens being warmed by a flickering lightbulb. I soon learn the space-age clear enclosures are now referred to as isolettes, not incubators, and they are designed to protect the most important things in the world: tiny, helpless, faultless babies.

In my day-to-day life, I'll admit I'm sometimes guilty of being unsympathetic, especially if I suspect someone's circumstances are the result of their own choices.

But this is an altogether different and striking scene. Even if you're a card-carrying, emotionless robot like me, that judgment just doesn't hold here. These are babies. Babies who have done nothing wrong, they haven't made any bad choices that put them here. These babies have done nothing to deserve their current circumstances. Take a look at just one of these amazing little humans, and you cannot cast an ounce of blame on them.

The NICU

I enter the semicircle of isolettes, and I am painfully aware that I am alone. Technically, there is still a nurse guiding me around and there are other staff in the room attending to the various babies, but I am amongst only strangers. I am in uncharted waters, about to absorb the most difficult thing I've ever viewed or experienced. There is no place I'd rather visit, because this is where my kids are, but I had never expected to need to be here. The nurse directs me to my left, and I am introduced to my daughter Eden for the second time in my life.

The reintroduction is surreal. She looks a lot different, all cleaned up.

Is this even her? She left so quickly; how can I know for sure? The fancy handwritten cardboard name tag on her isolette is correct, but that could have been misapplied too.

As these visions of conspiracy theories whisper in my subconscious I ask the nurse how they can be certain they've got the details correct. She reminds me how the wristbands were printed before the birth and applied immediately to Kylene and to each of the babies. I accept this is a reliable system, but you have to understand, having your babies pulled away so quickly, even if necessarily so, casts small shadows of concern, especially in situations saturated with stress.

Besides being cleaned up and perfectly adorable, the other factor fueling my line of questioning is that I just can't see her very well. She is transformed, almost unrecognizably, by a maze of equipment surrounding and connected to her body. Her face is obscured by a plastic bar with prongs extending across her tiny nose. There is a large brace and hose connected to her arm, a cuff on her leg, and countless other items I don't recognize or understand. Tubes, wires, monitors, machines, digital readouts, and chiming alarms.

In all my planning and forecasting, I had never imagined today being like this. Not the predawn phone call, the frantic drive home, the decision to deliver early, the surgery, all the blood, the babies, my need for orange juice, the insurance call, having three patients, and now all this gear hooked up to my tiny baby girl. The scene momentarily takes my breath away and is more than enough to break my heart. Questions fill my mind, sadness mixed with guilt and worry.

Why did this have to happen to her? Why can't I make this better? What if something else goes wrong?

These go unanswered and I barely have time to register any details before I am brought over to Roman who is a station away, with another baby between him and Eden.

"They're not together? Why are they not next to each other?" I query, confused and a little sad.

"These were the only open slots, and we don't just move a patient over unnecessarily," the nurse tries to explain.

But it is necessary. It seems so ridiculous to me. It would be much easier and more comforting for me to have them be side by side. I suppose if it were my baby in the middle, I wouldn't want her moved around, but let's be honest, the isolette is on wheels. How hard can it be? This day continues to tally one small heartache after another.

Roman is situated in his own isolette and is hooked up to all the same gear as his sister. A tube obscures his face, and he's connected to a mess of wires and sensors. My heart breaks again, overcome with the singeing pain of this new reality, the vast departure from my expectations, for what he's going through, and selfishly, for what I'm going through. He is so tiny, so helpless. They both are. And here I am, in my inaugural moments as a father, the role of a lifetime, the thing I've looked forward to most, and I've arrived ill-equipped to do anything remotely useful for them. I'm helpless; I am not in control, and I feel like a failure. But a proud failure, these are my babies, my son, and my daughter. I'm their dad.

Bringing in Mama

I wrestle with my new reality, our new reality, as I am bombarded by undulating waves of emotion. Joy for the absolute miracles of life before me, relief that they survived this far, fear for what they have left to endure and what their life will be like, and worry about… well, about everything.

I spend a few minutes, seeing, touching, and talking to each of them and taking in as much information as I can about each of their conditions and the care they are receiving. I am where I need to be, but I can't stay very long. I have another patient to visit, or rather, to rescue. Kylene's hour of mandatory rest in her room is nearly over and I know she will want to come see the kids.

Reversing course, I retrace my steps and make the journey out through the halls, down the elevator and back to Kylene's room. She is mentally ready to go, but understandably the staff won't let her walk yet, so they intend to push her whole bed. She's still in her hospital gown, only an hour removed from surgery, likely still having effects from the spinal, and in no shape to be traveling, but she is going. That much is certain. I imagine there is not much of anything that could stand in her way, and I certainly am not planning to try. Mama wants to see her babies, so off and up we go.

On the way, I try to explain and prepare her for what she's about to see. I relay my experience from the past hour, but nothing can truly prepare your heart to be broken in so many different ways and into so many pieces. As much as I love these two tiny miracles and have felt connected and involved throughout the entire pregnancy, Kylene has been with them more, they've literally been with her the whole time. They know her voice, her heartbeat, her everything. As hard as this day and first introduction has been for me, I'm sure it will be even worse for Kylene, not to mention that she's still enduring the lingering pain from the surgery and the shock of the last twenty-four hours. I fear that entering the NICU sanctum and seeing all the tubes, wires, monitors, and machines might push her over the edge. This first family meeting might be rough.

Our approach sequence unfolds just like it did my first time. The elevator doors glide open to a lobby of uncertainty for her, but this time, there is a small confidence of knowledge for me. I've done this before. I show her the wash-in station, explain the rules and after scrubbing thoroughly, we make our way down the hall for proper introductions.

I realize now that going in alone ahead of time was actually good for me, and good for us. I know where to go, what to do, what to expect, and I can prepare her. I have already entered the NICU and balanced the elation and suffering of the first sightings. This time, I can focus on being supportive and relay the knowledge I have already gained in hopes of being helpful to her as she survives her own first experience. Finally, I'm doing something somewhat useful.

We see Eden first and then Roman, with that order based purely on orientation of the room. Kylene tears up at both stations. Not loud, gasping, weeping tears, but tears leaking from the outside corners of her eyes and streaking down her cheeks. Yet, beyond those understandable tears, her eyes convey a host of other emotions: the light of relief, sparks of joy, a rush of undeniable love, and flickering hints of sadness. I can see and sense that she is experiencing the same realization I had on my visit to the NICU. These are our children, our precious babies, and this is their lot in life; right now, this is our path. It is a lot to accept and process all at once. There is also something new in Kylene, something recognizable but hard to define; a mix of innate tenderness and steely resolve reserved especially for mothers. From this moment forward, she is steadfastly focused on taking care of these babies.

Our hour with the babies is spent gently touching their heads and cheeks, letting their tiny hands hold our fingers, talking to them, and overreacting to every mildly distinguishable facial expression or movement they make. We find ourselves divided at their separate stations, each immersed in connection with one baby, when suddenly a pang of guilt arises and one of us says, "Do you want to switch?" And so, we switch spots, then after a while we switch again, starting what seems like an endless cycle of crisscrossing from one station to the other, each of us trying to give equal attention to both children. I lose track of time but really, time just stands still as we soak in the most precious moments of either of our lives until now. We are all here together, and as weird and unexpected as this setting is, I know I will never forget how I feel in this moment.

Soon we leave so Kylene can go back to her room to eat, rest, and recover. Leaving the room is hard, because though they are well cared for, these are our babies, and they are supposed to be with us.

Stay put guys, I'll be back soon.

All New Footage

From our first views of her in the NICU, Kylene and I can both plainly see that Eden's left foot was not "normal" after all which we confirm in discussions with her doctors. The concerns expressed during the ultrasounds had been correct—sort of. The good news is her foot isn't "club" or otherwise deformed. It's fully formed and functional with five perfect, tiny toes. The concerning part is that the foot is twisted outwardly to a noticeable extent, I'm guessing it's 120 degrees. The attending neonatologists and an orthopedic specialist suggest that she will need a brace, or a series of braces, and possibly surgery to correct the twist.

We are already overwhelmed, and this news delivers another devastating blow of heartache and disappointment. Then again, considering what other developmental challenges could be in front of us, and the fact that three hours ago I didn't know if she and her brother would be alive, it somehow seems manageable. Not simple, but manageable. The specialists outline plans for the future, but they seem far off and not that important at this time. For now, it is a new wrinkle in our increasingly complicated circumstances. We'll deal with it when the time comes.

Our pre-selected pediatrician visits Kylene's room to congratulate us and to inform us that he had already checked in at the NICU to meet his two newest patients. We know him well as he already sees both of us as adult patients, so his arrival is a buoyant force of positive energy. He gives a brief recitation on their respective conditions, what he expects is ahead, and what it all means. His calm explanations are reassuring and helpful, and somehow easier to receive coming from someone we know and trust. When I mention our growing concern over Eden's foot, he surprises us.

"Oh, that's just positional. I think her foot got stuck sideways because they were both so crammed in there. That will come right back around on its own in a few weeks. Don't worry about that at all."

Not worry? Easier said than done. He has just offered a completely different position than the legion of other opinions rendered thus far. Strangely, we are both taken aback by his outlying assessment, but we're encouraged by this new possibility. We briefly bask in the glow of potentially good news, cling to the new gift of hope his words bring, and savor the thought that maybe, just maybe, things are going to be okay.

Tour Guide

I feel like every room, every situation, and every conversation I've been thrust into today has been life-threatening or life-altering. I race from one situation to the next, my entire being saturated with tension. Exiting one room, I am surprised as I catch a glimpse of my parents in the hallway. Seeing them gives me a surge of happiness and lets me exhale as if I've been granted a temporary reprieve from my burdens.

There is nothing for them to do and they can't fix this situation, but they are here, and that's enough. I'm glad to see them, I'm eager to share with them more details of what has happened so far, to express how excited I am to be a dad, and to commiserate over the difficult days, weeks, and possibly years ahead. They are each bearing smiles, facades of happiness and anticipation, but their eyes and the tightness of their hugs belie a poorly concealed secret. They are draped in cloaks of worry. Worry for their son and daughter-in-law, still in our 20s, suddenly bearing the weight of the world. Worry for grandchildren they haven't even met yet, born too early and with a forecast of struggle.

They aren't the only visitors. After getting Kylene to the hospital and standing vigil with her until I arrived, Katie had been assigned to make notifications of what was happening, and she came through in spades. She sounded the alarm, far and wide, announcing the early arrival, and high-level concern for the twins' well-being.

Now, the alert is out, and people are coming to the hospital to see us. Well, not to see me so much, but everyone else in our recently expanded family.

They each receive the news over the phone and are excited for us, but the unique circumstances sow seeds of concern and leave many unanswered questions. Are the babies okay? Is Kylene okay? What is happening? What happens next? Incomplete, short-term answers are all that Katie could offer. That's not her fault, we just don't have many answers yet, so there's nothing more to share.

They come anyway, even without answers, or perhaps because there are none. They stop what they are doing and just start coming, without the benefit of details, without knowing much of anything other than the babies are here and they might be in trouble.

Kylene's mom, Kylene's dad and stepmom, our siblings, and even some friends have come. I can't tell you the order of who arrived first, and they don't always stay very long, but they have started to arrive in steady succession.

They come, and they are here, and there is nothing for them to do but just be present, simply as a sign of support. Family support for us and our babies. I don't express it well, or at all really, but the support is appreciated, welcomed, and somehow sustaining. I'm thankful for all of it.

However, these visitors aren't here only to wave flags of solidarity. They are all secretly, or not so secretly, hopeful to see and meet the babies. As a proud father, I'm more than happy to oblige the requests, but obviously this comes with some challenges. The babies aren't here in the room with Kylene so there is no customary scene of everyone crowding around a bassinet. There is no gazing through the hallway window into an infant nursery with a gaggle of other eager onlookers. Our babies aren't even on the same floor where they might have been if things were different, if they had come a month later. They are in a different place. It will take a little effort, but the coordination hurdles are not a deterrent for eager grandparents, aunts, or uncles, and so, within the first few hours of the twins' arrival, the escorted tours to the NICU begin.

The rules of engagement for visiting the NICU suddenly become more relevant and important. Visitors must always be accompanied by a parent, the patient visitor limit is a total of four at one time, and there are no kids allowed. Given we have twins, I thought there may be grounds for manipulating rule technicalities and insisting that I should actually be allowed to have a total of eight visitors at a time. I'm told no, and I don't push it. As for the numbers, I also learn that the escorting parent counts as one of the four, so it's really three visitors at a time. This isn't a problem either, but it means that it takes some time to rotate everyone in. And, since Kylene is still recovering in her room, I am the one and only approved NICU escort and thus have just been promoted to head tour guide.

Three by three, I take the interested family members to meet the twins and guide them through the physical and emotional aspects of the process. The stages are just like I had done alone, and then with Kylene, but now I can be the knowledgeable docent, providing an experienced perspective on this unfamiliar place. I lead them up the elevator, through the scrubbing procedure, down the hall, and then I always stop just outside the room.

Here is where I advise them of what they are about to see. Having been through this myself, I feel it is important to manage expectations and prepare them as adequately as possible. Despite how beautiful, precious, and deeply loved these babies are, this is not a typical infant introduction, and it is a lot to take in and process. The babies are tiny, just over three pounds each. This is less than half the weight of most newborns. They are not chubby with rolls at their knees and elbows. Rather, they are quite thin, in a way you've probably never seen a baby before. Then, there is the equipment, lots of it, and it is a little overwhelming and obscuring, and might even make you a little sad. Lastly, I usually feel compelled to mention Eden's foot. Though we have renewed hope for a natural correction of this condition, the current view is somewhat startling as the twist is noticeable and a little unsettling.

With these expectations set, there is another gut punch I must deliver: the contact rules. NICU policies insist that unless you're a grandparent, you can't touch the babies, and even that is minimal. If the limited contact rules were not restrictive enough, Kylene and I also called an audible on our first visit together. The NICU rules actually state that only parents and grandparents may *hold* the babies. However, extending this opportunity to pick them up is of course up to the discretion of the parents. Kylene and I, in a state of extreme caution and maybe even shock, are worried about the very lives of our kids, and decided to permit only the two of us, the parents, to hold the babies. Any other physical contact is hence limited strictly to grandparents. We don't want to hurt anyone's feelings, but we also don't want to extend unnecessary risk to the kids and with so many grandparents, we decide to just play it safe. We levy this restriction with a half-truth and just blame the NICU for the rule. Sorry mom and dad. It isn't you, it's me.

Even with all the surprises and the rules and the unique circumstances, I find that each new introduction to Roman and Eden is special. My mom and dad are early in the rotation, and they carry a mix of emotions. Smiles and happiness stirred with compassion, worry and pain. Most of their time is spent putting a finger in the isolette and holding the babies' tiny hands. They take lots of pictures, and converse with the newborns offering endless baby-talk and other expressions of endearment. They too embrace the moment for what it is and avoid mourning what it isn't. Though this is not how any of us expected this day to go, this is our reality: these are my children, these are their grandchildren, and this is the moment. It is painful and wonderful at the same time.

Kylene's dad and stepmom come up and I give them the preparation speech. After mentioning Eden's foot, Kylene's stepmom looks right at me and without skipping a beat says,

"Oh, we can fix feet."

Her calm delivery is soothing and serves as a reminder for me. She's right. It might not be easy, but we *can* fix it. Once they come in and meet the kids, they settle right into being mesmerized. They are a quieter pair, but with no less love for their kids and grandkids than my parents. They too struggle balancing the joy and worry, but clearly enjoy their time and the blessings they are witnessing.

My sister comes up and has lots of questions, but really, she just wants to be here, to meet Roman and Eden. As she describes it, her eyes leak a little when she first sees them, but I think she is more happy than sad.

This soon becomes the norm as various iterations of this routine continue all evening and into the coming days. Most come with wonder and apprehension, then leave with some remaining concerns, but also with some overarching sense of joy. Some are understandably unsettled by the equipment, or the twisted foot, or they are simply overwhelmed with worry and empathy. A few even opt to leave the room to steady themselves and, truly, I cast no judgment. I understand completely.

It's a hard thing, gazing down on someone you love so much, fearing they are struggling, feeling helpless to do anything for them, wanting to take away the pain, and make sure they will be okay. It's emotionally taxing, but all of these visitors are willing to subject themselves to this out of love for us and our babies.

It's a difficult place to visit, and yet I come again and again, bringing dozens of people in for a glimpse and an introduction. So many trips with so many people who love and care about my kids. It's exhilarating and exhausting. It's the hardest thing I've ever had to do, and I keep doing it over and over and over. But there is no place I'd rather be.

Raspberry Cinnamon Swirl

Late in the day, I finally find a moment to take a break from running visiting tours and flop down in the guest chair in Kylene's patient room. There on the small side table is an untouched grocery bag of food that my mom brought when she first arrived at the hospital several hours ago. I had forgotten about the bag before, but with the wave of visitors now subsided, I quickly realize I'm absolutely starving. Digging into the contents of the bag, I find an assortment of granola bars and a banana, but the thing monopolizing the volume of the bag is the pièce de résistance: an entire loaf of bread.

I haul it out and begin to examine the prize. Even through the transparent plastic bag, it is clear this is no ordinary bread. The label says this is raspberry cinnamon swirl bread, and it looks incredible. I hastily remove the twist-tie, open the bag, and am engulfed by a sweet aroma.

Mom's bag of essentials includes a knife as well, so I waste no time and cut off a slice, in the process rendering my hands sticky with sugary glaze and raspberry filling. I stuff a bite into my mouth and stop short.

Oh my goodness.

Perhaps it is due to my hours of sustained adrenaline, my overall heightened state of mind, or my unintended day of fasting, but the first bite is glorious. Truly unlike anything I've encountered in quite some time. It is almost embarrassing how much I am enjoying this bread. One slice turns into two, and then three, and each bite is just as satisfying as the one before.

I am grateful to my mom, but not at all surprised. Mom has always been the unquestionable center of gravity of my immediate family, and one of the forces that pulls us together is her meals. They are good and hearty, the epitome of comfort food. Allspice seasoning on a slow-cooking beef roast is the smell of every Sunday dinner of my childhood. A hand mixer grinding up mashed potatoes and stirring in the butter is the accompanying soundtrack.

If we are not gathered at my parents' house or cottage, Mom always makes or buys something and brings the food with her to wherever we are. There is always something to eat, just in case we need it, and today she knew how much I would need this. She knew I would be too busy caring for my wife and new babies to find food for myself, and so she did what she could—what she has always done--to take care of me.

Thanks, Mom.

How Are You Doing?

So many of our family and friends have come, and in a seemingly steady stream. Some are expected, some are a surprise, but each sign of support is appreciated, more than those people will ever know. We are blessed to have so many people who care about us. They all come and take the tour, they all visit Kylene in her room, many bring gifts, and they all ask how she and the babies are doing.

At some point, if they remember that I'm there too, they ask me how I am doing. But I don't have the strength, the clarity, or the right words to answer truthfully. I usually just report that I am fine and deflect any questions and concerns to the well-being of the babies and Kylene. I typically insert the quip that I didn't do anything, which is true. I didn't have surgery; I just sat in the room and nearly passed out. I didn't nearly die in utero and require extraction in emergency fashion; I just sat in the room and needed orange juice. I'm not the one with a headache from where my spinal fluid is dripping out of my spinal column. I'm not a three-pound baby, surviving as a miracle of providence through modern science. I'm not the one hooked to a mess of wires and tubes. I'm not the one experiencing any of these things, so I conclude that I'm fine. That's what I tell anyone who asks anyway. I'm *fine*. Maybe a little tired, but I'm fine and thanks for asking. But I'm not fine.

My lifelong dream of becoming a father is coming true. It's wonderful, but it is also taxing, to say the least. I'm barely holding it together.

It started as an earthquake shaking my entire reality, testing the foundations of everything I know. I am absolutely disturbed and damaged and in fear of aftershocks. But I am not a damaged building.

The earthquake also triggered an avalanche, releasing a slide to tumble down the precarious slope of a mountain, transporting immeasurable amounts of debris, fear, and worry. But I am not the mountainside buried below the detritus of the avalanche.

At its final crescendo, the avalanche cascaded snow, rocks, and uprooted trees into a pristine alpine lake, displacing millions of gallons of water, erupting the serene glass surface into a series of towering concentric waves which sweep outward in all directions, disrupting every square inch of the lake surface, and raising the water levels to record heights. But I am not the disturbed lake.

At the far end of the suddenly swollen lake is a narrow, aged concrete hydroelectric dam. The dam holds back the water, creating the lake, but simultaneously lets water through and regulates the flow. It was always meant for control, organized management of water, and the electrical power it produces. Now the surging waters are lapping at its crest, micro-fissures form in the exposed concrete face and threaten to escalate into cracks and gaps. The dam withstands the onslaught, endures against the greatest test since its construction, perhaps being pushed beyond what it was ever designed for. Strain consumes every fiber; Every molecule is at the threshold of failure. An aura of distress surrounds the entire barricade, with a palpable perception of fatigue and trembling. One more aftershock, one more sliding snowflake, one more ripple of change in the water, and the dam may very well lose control and burst.

I am the dam.

Home Alone

As this seemingly endless day dwindles down past evening, my parents, the nurses, and even Kylene encourage me to go home to get some rest, but I want to stay. My whole world, everything that matters to me most, is in this hospital, and I need to be here.

The rounding doctor on Kylene's floor graciously contends,

"The babies are under twenty-four-hour care, and your wife needs to rest. There is nothing for you to do tonight. If you stay, you won't sleep well and all that will do is run you down further. Then you'll get sick, and then you're no good to anyone. They will need you soon. Go home and sleep."

She has a point, several good points, actually. But there must be a call room or an empty patient room somewhere for me to crash in. All I need is a bed.

When I raise this idea to staff, it is made abundantly clear to me that despite my willingness and creativity, that isn't happening. I can't just sleep in an empty bed anywhere I can find a spot; there are rules.

Technically, I can just sleep in a chair in Kylene's room, but that option does make me hesitate. When we came in a few weeks ago, I slept in the chair in her room, steadfastly by her side, and, I must admit, the accommodations were less than stellar. Every fathomable sleeping position was uncomfortable, there was lots of noise, and there were constant interruptions. I learned my lesson on the chair-sleeping vigil.

After much encouragement, I start to relent as I think back on the last twenty-four hours in mass sum. The ill-advised late-night *Spanglish* viewing, the autobahn-esqe drive from Indiana, the bombardment of unexpected information, the blood, the birth, the foot, the countless tours through the NICU, and the likelihood that I may have two months of this ahead of me.

I need to shower, I need clean clothes, I need some normal food, and Kylene has a list of things she wants as well.

Most of all, I desperately need to sleep.

They are right. I need to go home.

I pack up my things, say goodnight to Kylene, take my validated parking ticket from the nursing station and head to the parking garage. The walk seems endless, as I trudge out alone and utterly exhausted. It's surreal how much has changed since I hurriedly parked my truck here less than ten hours ago. It's as if the world doesn't know just how pivotal today has been. I arrived here as one person and I leave now forever changed. There are no more preceding modifiers. No more "expectant" or "soon-to-be." I'm a father. The greatest title I'll ever attain.

Everything feels different, but pulling out and leaving the hospital thrusts me back into the realities of traffic, late November weather, and the rest of the world that seems to be rolling along just fine without me. I mindlessly drive home, park in the garage, walk in the door to an empty house, and I'm struck by a gaping void. I am alone. I'm not supposed to come home alone like this. I'm supposed to have my wife and our babies with me. But they're not with me. They're not here and I'm not there and I'm again having trouble reconciling the unbalanced variables of my life equation. I recommit myself once again to the goal of being ready. I have to be ready for when they do need me, and no one knows how soon that will be.

I amble up the stairs toward our bedroom, but instead of turning right to the master suite, I turn left to their room. The nursery, painted green, with light tan carpet and two white wooden cribs in opposite corners. The letters, "R" and "E," decorate the walls above the head ends of each crib. The furniture includes a tall white dresser and a beige plush upholstered glider with matching gliding ottoman for feeding and rocking babies. I stand in the doorway and am moved to pray.

I pray out loud, thanking God for my wife and children, desperately begging for them to be okay, and pleading for them to come home soon. As I conclude, I say one final thing out loud to the empty room, to the place where they are *supposed* to be, where I want them to be, and where I'm convinced they will be someday soon. It feels strange but good as it rolls out of my mouth, perhaps for the first time, but certainly not the last.

"I love you guys."

Part VII - Stress

Holding Pattern

(Day 2 in the NICU)

I awaken to my alarm and as I clear the cobwebs from my mind, I'm reminded of what happened over the last twenty-four hours.

Oh, right. Everything has changed. The babies have arrived, I'm a dad now. I need to get back to the hospital.

Kylene and I agreed last night on what time I would return so we can go up to the NICU together. I quickly shower, get dressed, grab the things Kylene had wanted from the house, including the camera, and I hop in the truck. Our house is less than fifteen minutes from the hospital, so it's a short drive, and significantly less frenetic than my trek yesterday.

I find Kylene in her room and she is waiting for me. Never mind the pain of recovery from surgery less than a day ago, she is ready to go. We head up to the NICU as quickly as I can get her up there, and we plan to stay as long as they'll let her remain out of her room. She is still a patient and really should recover herself, but the nurses and doctors understand her need to be there.

We work our way through the required arrival routine, removing watches, washing up to our elbows, and once dried and reassembled, we head down the hall, take a left, and left again into their room. Of course, I know there are a lot of babies in here, and lots of stories beginning, but nevertheless I think of it as *their* room. Arriving in the room today has fewer surprises than yesterday, and the enormity of the situation no longer feels overwhelming. Not as much anyway.

The isolettes are in the same places, the equipment is the same, and everything is more or less the way it was yesterday. Roman and Eden are still wrapped in typical hospital blankets, white with blue and pink striping, and their heads are topped with handmade hats provided by an army of volunteer retired ladies who donate their time and resources for tiny babies they don't even know.

The nurses walk us through the status updates on each baby, tell us that they did well in the night, and then let us begin our second day of parenthood.

One of us remembers to get out the camera and now we have something new to focus on. I take overall shots while Kylene starts experimenting with special filtered black and white poses. The customary hand wrapped around a finger photo. Closeups of their feet. Dozens of photos. Maybe hundreds. Altogether too many, and yet somehow not enough.

With every single possible photo taken, we take a break, and each choose a station to resume growing our relationships with our children. Gentle talking, touching their hands and feet, and overreacting to every muscle twitch and audible sound they offer.

"Did you see that? She's smiling."

"Come look at this. He's pouting."

"I think her eyebrow just moved a fraction of a millimeter."

And so on. It might sound ridiculous to anyone else, but for us it is intoxicating and perfectly wonderful. It's almost enough to make us forget where we are and relieve some of the stress of being in this room. We might be able to forget entirely, if not for the tangled cords or and beeping monitors that go off every few minutes and yank us out of moments of pure joy and back into reality. Then we switch spots, each to the other baby, because there's always someone to give attention to, and we do it all over again. And then we switch again. And again.

At some point during one of my shifts at Eden's station, the nurse asks me,

"Would you like to hold her?"

A little surprised, I reply, "I didn't know that I could."

"Of course you can."

"Well, then yes."

Neither of us had even asked yesterday. With all the equipment, I had assumed there were too many entanglements and too much risk, so as much as I have been wanting to hold my daughter and my son, I just want them to be ok, so I hadn't even asked yet. I should have asked. I missed a day of contact with my kids. That ends now.

The nurse gets me situated in a chair next to Eden's isolette and gently lifts her out of the vessel. All the cords and hoses are long enough, and we are careful to make sure nothing gets caught as she places Eden in my arms, all three pounds of her. She is so small and fairly obscured by all the gear, but she is alive, breathing and wiggling around, and she's absolutely perfect. I steal a glance at Kylene who is holding Roman and having the same experience. After everything we endured yesterday, this is a nice surprise, an unexpected gift of a moment to be treasured. After many minutes we finally relinquish the babies back to their isolettes to let them rest. I could hold Eden all day, but I know she needs to sleep unabated.

A little while later, we each get to repeat the experience with the other baby. I get to hold Roman for the first time and it is just as exhilarating. Another gift today.

There are more visitors, some repeats from yesterday and other new ones that couldn't come before. My tour guide duties resume, but I'm okay with that role. This is my life right now, this is where I am, this is where my kids are, and I'm excited to introduce everyone to them. They are my everything and I'm proud to share that news with anyone who will listen.

Sound Judgment

Roman and Eden are having their routine hearing tests today. We didn't know when she was coming, but now the audiology technician is here, and she glides right in with testing equipment on a rolling cart. Roman is up first. After gently placing a soft earphone in each of his ears and some sensors on his head to record his responses, the technician applies some clicks and other sounds and then documents the results. It only takes a few minutes and then she repeats the whole sequence on Eden.

"Roman passed the test," reports the audiology technician, "but Eden failed the test in one ear." She shares the information of the failure very casually, as if she were a waitress relaying the condiment options at the salad bar. This isn't casual information to me! She probably doesn't know about Eden's foot, or what we've just been through in the last forty-eight hours, or how heavy this is all weighing on us, but this new wrinkle is not welcome news.

My mind races to process what the results might mean.

Is she deaf? Will she be able to speak properly? Is this correctable? Do we need cochlear implants? What will her life be like?

My poor baby girl, life has barely even started and already there is such hardship on the horizon. *What else can go wrong?*

As the tech wraps up her report and prepares to leave, she mentions the failed test again. Only this time she elaborates, explaining,

"By the way, over fifty percent of the tests I do end up with a false negative reading, so I wouldn't worry too much about those results."

Um, okay. Now I have even more questions. What kind of testing system is this? Is this equipment error or user error? What good is the test if it is wrong more often than it's right? What in the world is going on here?

I have so many statistical and operational concerns with the whole testing protocol that my head is spinning. This is bad, comically bad, and it's so bad I don't even know what to do with it. I'm not quite as worried as I was, but now I'm doubting the validity of Roman's test. The technician is just doing her job, and works with the equipment she has, but seriously. That was the single worst possible scenario for any test. He passed, but she failed, but the test isn't very reliable at all. The solution? She will come back in two days and rerun the test.

For what purpose? Presumably, to make sure Eden passes. If the results are meaningless the first time, different results two days later don't have a different or better meaning either, right? Right?

Two days later, Eden passes the second test, so now there is no problem at least according to the method. This is obviously scientific nonsense; I want to throw my hands up with that test but instead I just shake my head.

Whatever. I'll just run my own tests.

I talk to Eden right near her face and ears and see if she responds. I'm pretty sure she can hear me.

Need to Know

Over the next few visits, as I repeatedly come into the NICU and continue getting more comfortable being here, I start really paying attention to what is going on and how the nurses perform their tasks. Mainly, my focus centers on all of the equipment, all the monitors and all the devices. These machines are monitoring and, to some degree, sustaining the life of my children. I want to know what each item is, what it does, and how it works.

Between escorting our friends and family to see the babies and the many personal bedside visits, I spend hours in this room each day, staring absently at monitors and trying to figure out what everything means, willing the readings to improve—or in some cases, stay where they are even though I don't really know what a good or bad reading looks like. My obsession and attentiveness are not lost on anyone, least of all the nurses who do their best to field my questions.

For my engineering mind, or perhaps just to feed my controlling nature, I want to know the meaning behind every seemingly nebulous alarm or chiming monitor. I want to know more. I *need* to know more. If I know how it works, I might know if it's working correctly. More importantly, if I know how it works and what it really means, the alarms might not be so scary. My hope is that eventually I can differentiate between what really is a problem and what isn't.

Right now, I interpret every beep, chime, or flashing light to mean one of my kids is in danger, and my anxiety spikes every time something happens. Double babies means double the alarms, and lights, and therefore, double the anxiety. It feels like a constant deluge of warnings that I don't understand. Without knowing what they mean, I always assume the worst, and the endless visions of peril are slowly eroding my soul. I need to know more or I'm going to go insane.

In my normal spheres of work and life, when I want to know things, I ask questions. That sounds obvious, that's what everyone does, right? No, not like I do. I ask more questions than the normal person. In this singular instance, and trust me, it doesn't happen often, I think Kylene would agree with me. She would tell you that even in social situations, I can carry (or force) a much longer conversation because if I'm interested, I keep asking questions. More questions. Probing for more depth, detail, and understanding. This is how I connect and how I get comfortable. It helps me to become relatable and understand the intricacies of the situation.

Lately, when people ask me what I do for a living, and I begin to describe my work as an investigative engineer, I have started to distill it down to a simple phrase, a motto I've tried to adopt and apply to my life.

Help people solve problems.

I change the punctuation sometimes, and while it doesn't substantially change the meaning, maybe it shifts the emphasis a little.

Help people. Solve problems.

My job is solving problems. Sometimes they are easy, but more often they are complex, with multiple changing variables, nuances that take time to understand, and situational context that colors all facets of the issues. What I've come to realize is every problem, regardless of its breadth or complexity, is a compound of multiple smaller problems. The more I can understand all aspects of an issue, the more I can break things down into smaller, manageable sub-problems. Then I can hopefully start solving the big problem one small problem at a time.

This extended moment, the one I'm living right now in the NICU, is the most foundationally challenging situation of my life. It is a tangled mess of problems, wrapped in an interconnected, multi-layered mesh of unknowns. Naturally, I have started things off as I often do, by asking questions. I ask lots of questions, and they are directed at whichever unsuspecting nurse has the misfortune of being in my vicinity when a question comes to mind.

It generally goes something like this.

"What is this device?" I ask, gesturing to the item wrapped around my daughter's foot.

"That's the pulse ox," replies the nurse who has unknowingly been caught in my web of inquiry.

Great, now I know the name of the contraption. Not really helpful.

"What does it do?" I query further.

"It monitors the oxygen level in the blood," the nurse responds.

Factual, yet still inadequate for me.

"Yes, but how does it work?"

"We attach this cuff to her ankle, and it takes the reading."

Literal and descriptive, yet still lacking.

"I understand that's how you attach it, but how does it actually work? *How* does it read the oxygen levels?"

An extended series of back-and-forth responses ensues, with no new technical information provided to quell my intrigue, and soon, with a mild level of frustration mounting, the exchange concludes as the fatigued nurse relinquishes with her final salvo,

"I can't answer your questions."

Indeed, she cannot, because she doesn't know the answers, and honestly, I probably shouldn't expect her to know how the machines actually work. I'm not trying to impugn her personally or come across harshly; I'm simply trying to unravel the challenge in front of me. My non-malicious intent doesn't mean it's any less exhausting though. She knows how to set up the equipment and how to respond to their respective readings. She's a nurse, not a mechanical engineer, and I'm probably being a little unfair expecting her to answer my endless stream of questions.

Still, I'd like to know more. No, I need to know more, and I was desperately hoping she could help me. More questions will come as I can't hold out forever, but I've stopped for now to recalibrate my angle of attack. It's only a matter of time. There should be a note in the twins' medical charts: "WARNING. Be advised, dad is an engineer." In fact, I highly suspect something like that *is* in the chart. Or if it isn't, it soon will be.

I remain dissatisfied with the content of the answers I am receiving, so I end up turning to other means and I begin to scour the internet for information. I find various medical sites that appear relevant and dependable and soon begin to glean a better understanding of what all this gear surrounding my children is actually doing. Finally, some answers.

CPAP

First, there is the ubiquitous CPAP tubing. CPAP is an acronym for Continuous Positive Airway Pressure. You've probably heard of it before just maybe in a different context. It is a common respiratory support method that many adults use to prevent snoring and sleep apnea. You know that Darth Vader mask on the nightstand? Right. One of those things. This version of CPAP is generally the same idea, but slightly different in that it's used in neonatal units to assist newborn babies with their breathing. The baby version provides a continuous flow of pressurized air to the baby's lungs, helping to keep their airways open, preventing lung collapse, and preventing the surfaces from sticking together. The steroid injections Kylene had a few weeks before the babies were born was to promote surfactant development and usher in a massive lung performance improvement.

It seems to have worked. They are both breathing quite well, and they are actually ahead of normal development progress at this gestation. I never thought I'd be thankful for those two stressful days and long uncomfortable nights a few weeks ago, but the more I learn, the more I realize those doses of steroids likely made our road a lot smoother now. Steroids might have saved my kids' lives.

All that success made their lungs work better, and it means the CPAP pressure is quite low—they barely need it. Nevertheless, they do have it, at least for a little while. So, while I celebrate their positive circumstances, we still have the tubes with little prongs that slide into their tiny nostrils to deliver the pressurized air, and then the tube is secured with tape to prevent dislodgement. That all makes perfect sense… until you see tape stuck to your baby's face. It turns my stomach. There is tape stuck to the perfect skin on my kids' cheeks, and the tubes extend across the upper lip, just under the nose. Their faces are already so small, and these tubes obscure the view a lot. Not their view of the world from their eyes, thankfully, but our view of them. This delivers an additional source of pain for me.

When you have a new baby, all you want to do is to look at them and carefully inspect every perfect molecule, every dimple, every eyelash. You marvel at every twitch, every pout, and everything that remotely looks like a smile. I am no different, except my babies are even smaller and more precious. I still want to look at them, study every square inch, and soak in their perfection. The tubes are large and visible, clearly the most noticeable item on their bodies and I suspect the most irritating for them. I can't see the entire face of either of my babies. Plus, the tape must be itchy and must tug at their skin. If I pretend that it doesn't bother them, even if it's not irritating to them (but how can it not be?), it is still irritating for me to have to look at. I want to see my children's faces without obstruction and without any tape. Ergo, I hate the CPAP.

Pulse Ox

Around one foot, each baby has a small white plastic cuff with a Velcro fastener. The cuff has a small red dot of electronic light that points inward toward the skin and a ribbon of connecting wires that trail off to some unknown destination. This item is what all the nursing staff refer to as the pulse ox, the pulse oximeter.

More internet scouring sent me tumbling down a rabbit hole where I learned the origins of pulse oximetry come from John Lambert in the 1700s whose findings in spectrometry caused him to be revered as a polymath.

(*What in the world is a Polymath?* It comes from the Greek of "having learned much," mixed with the Latin of "universal human." Perhaps we engineers, to counteract the disparaging social notions, should be so celebrated. From now on, I'd prefer if everyone just refers to me as a universal human.)

Anyway, the Lambert guy figured out a lot of things that are now helping my kids. The workings of the pulse ox are centered on the concepts of light absorption and different light wavelengths. The little red light on the thin Velcro cuff measures the oxygen saturation of the blood, thereby determining how well the lungs are working, which all circles back to the CPAP.

Now, would that have been so hard to convey? It's pretty simple. I feel like the nurse could have given me an abridged dissertation at the very least. Maybe just a brief PowerPoint presentation with a few visual graphics touching on the highlights. I can't be the only NICU parent looking for a comprehensive lecture about the esteemed polymath Lambert and his work from hundreds of years ago, right? Okay, it's probably just me.

The IV

Each baby, on one of their arms, has a large contraption that looks like a splint for a broken limb. In actual dimensions, it's quite small, but relatively speaking, the bar takes up a large piece of real estate on their tiny baby arms. Their arm isn't actually broken or twisted; the splint is only a stabilizer for the needle that pokes into a blood vessel.

The needle is the initial delivery end of an intravenous supply line, better known as an IV. Technically, the needle doesn't stay in there forever, the plastic catheter does, but it starts with a needle in the first place. Intravenous fluids are an absolute necessity right now as they supply hydration, food in the form of liquid nutrient nourishment, and any medicines that are needed. The need for an IV is clear to me. Their little bodies are supposed to still be inside the uterus, with an umbilical cord supplying everything: food, water, and even oxygen. But now that they are out of the uterus, the umbilical cords are gone, and things need to be managed differently. They aren't ready to be feeding yet. They can't take a bottle or nurse traditionally, as their suck-swallow-breathe reflex isn't expected to develop for several more weeks.

Think of a time when you've taken a drink, and you accidentally got the water "down the wrong pipe." We have all done it. The traffic control trap door in your throat, the epiglottis, falls asleep at his post and accidentally lets the water down the breathing pipe (brachial branch) instead of down into your stomach. You know immediately what has happened, and your brain sends all sorts of alarm signals to resolve the mistake. A rousing fit of coughing occurs, and your body usually self-stabilizes within a minute or two. The occurrence is surprising because it doesn't happen that often. It doesn't happen because your brain doesn't let it happen. Your brain reflexively knows how to close off the airway, suck the water in, swallow the water, and reopen the airway to breathe. It happens rapidly, repeatedly, and without any conscious input.

Premature infants haven't yet had that class in their formative brain development curriculum. It usually occurs somewhere in the range of 32-35 weeks of gestation, when most babies are still in utero. Roman and Eden were born early, at 30 weeks and 6 days, so that part of their brains hasn't developed yet.

It is fascinating really, the detail with which modern medicine understands human development. Except that when it's your kids, and you're staring at a calendar filled with a bunch of "not until" reasons that your kids can't do something, or can't try something, it is also frustrating and concerning at the same time.

I know why the IV is there and how important it is. I know it's necessary and helpful. But it is still a needle in my baby's arm. One each in both of my babies to be exact. Sigh.

Phototherapy

Both Roman and Eden also have elevated levels of a chemical called bilirubin in their blood. Bilirubin is created by the body naturally as it breaks down old red blood cells. Then, the liver removes the bilirubin, and your body excretes it as waste.

Babies often have issues with a buildup of bilirubin because their livers aren't functioning perfectly right at birth. Outwardly, the bilirubin buildup causes a yellow color in the skin and the whites of eyes. The resulting condition is referred to as jaundice. Most relevant websites indicate nearly sixty percent of full-term newborns have jaundice, but nearly eighty percent of preemies have it. The most concerning issue here is that if bilirubin levels get too high and crosses the blood brain barrier (a network of blood vessels and tissue that helps keep harmful substances from reaching the brain) it can result in damage. Usually it's not a problem, but it's important stuff.

Even though this is yet another thing for them to have to deal with, jaundice seems to be the one thing I've heard of before. I know it's pretty common, and for that reason, despite some potential dire possibilities, it doesn't worry me as much as some of the other stuff. I think the known is less scary than the unknown. Helping further is the realization that our twins' jaundice cases are not severe. Even so, the bilirubin levels are high enough that they do require phototherapy treatment with bili lights.

Bili lights are specialized lamps that emit a specific wavelength of light that helps to break down bilirubin in the baby's body. The babies' clothes are removed, leaving only their diaper, so that their skin can be exposed, but they have special wrap-around sunglasses to protect their eyes. When exposed under these lights for an extended period of time, the bilirubin in their skin absorbs the light and undergoes a chemical reaction, converting it into a form that can be easily excreted from the body. It's generally a simple concept and execution.

I have to admit, the protective glasses are kind of silly and look sort of cute on their little heads. My tiny little movie stars. Maybe it's because I know the phototherapy doesn't hurt and the glasses don't hurt that I'm able to be more calm about this treatment. This is the one piece of equipment that doesn't make me sad or frustrated. I understand it, it's not severe, and it's a very short-term issue. Problem identified, problem explained, and the problem is on its way to being resolved.

Heart monitors

Like all their other pieces and parts, the babies' hearts have been developing nearly since conception and have been actually beating since the third week of gestation. What started visually a barely perceptible flickering on the ultrasound screen later became that whooshing sound that I delighted in hearing several months ago. The heart is the universal initial indicator of life and remains the consistent metronome of living until the day we each expire. Proper, consistent, reliable heart function is foundational to surviving and thriving, in all facets of the human existence. The NICU is no exception.

The twins each have their own electrocardiogram (ECG or EKG) monitors, often just referred to as a heart monitor. These monitors use electrodes placed on the baby's chest to detect the electrical activity of the heart, records and displays each heartbeat, report the real time heart rate, and monitor the trends of functionality. The electrodes consist of a pair of thin transmission wire leads that terminate at a sensor about the size of nickel. The electrode sensors are adhered directly to the baby's skin with a small sticky pad. These pads get dirty or otherwise worn out every few days and are regularly replaced. The wire leads are gathered together and fed down under the baby's shirt and out their pant legs, so, if they're clothed, the leads are somewhat out of sight. If they happen to be in just their diapers, you can clearly see the wires and where they're stuck on the bare skin.

Critically important, but simple to comprehend. My two key takeaways: First, the heart needs to keep beating and so we monitor it continuously. Second, preemie heart rates are really high compared to what we're used to with adults. They are like hummingbirds. Don't be concerned by those high numbers.

Alarming

With the functional purposes finally somewhat understood, my focus shifts to the sounds made by the equipment. The alarms.

What does that alarm mean? What does that beeping mean? Is that bad? Well, it certainly doesn't seem good.

More and more questions from me lead to more answers from doctors and nurses that don't quite satisfy my curiosity. This leads to deeper explanations from some and short responses from others with better things to do than placate the rambling idiot.

Still, it is important to me to know. I gain confidence in knowing and can relax an iota or two. Understanding the alarms is important, because, with my minimal accumulation of meaningful comprehension on the topic, the alarms are still, well, alarming. By definition it seems like they should be. So, I begin to surveil the level of urgency of the nursing response to each of the alarms. I notice which sounds cause an immediate reaction, which command only a moderate reaction, and those that go ignored entirely. That's right ignored. At least that's how it seems, and it kind of drives me crazy.

Something is beeping over here, isn't that a problem? Isn't this concerning? Shouldn't it be? Is somebody going to do something?

After what seems like hours, but is likely only minutes, or even seconds, a nurse finally notices the alarm and ambles over, touches a button on the screen to silence the alarm, checks on his condition, and, when she is satisfied nothing is wrong, casually returns to her work.

I would really like to see more expediency. I'm worried about everything, and unaddressed alarms only fuel my worry further. Why is her response so relaxed?

I guess I can concede that technically the alarm has stopped, and everything seems okay with my kid, but I'm still not thrilled about her reaction time. It happens again about twenty minutes later, and then again. This cycle repeats again and again. Alarm, response. Alarm, response. Alarm, long wait, response. Alarm, two alarms of differing tones, response. Sometimes I ask if things are okay or ask the nurse to check, and sometimes I will myself to stay quiet, biting my tongue in mental agony, silently screaming for someone to help my baby or at least turn off that incessant beeping.

Eventually, I start to sort things out. The IV alarm is just telling us the bag is empty and the liquid delivery of nutrients has ended. This sound is a notification, and not truly an alarm and not a cause of concern. The other dings, chimes and other sounds come from various contraptions, but based on my many hours of observation and incognito data collection, I realize those are generally harmless as well.

I eventually conclude that the main item of concern is really the heart monitor. This one screen conveys critical information that is fairly easy to understand, but that simplicity is hindered by constant fluctuations. It signals good one moment and spells despair the next, and then back again. Calm, panic, relief, calm, calm, panic, extreme panic, relief. This sequence summarizes about a thirty second window of my day. This is my station in life: meticulously monitoring. I am monitoring the monitor, as if my watching the monitor somehow changes things. It doesn't, but here I sit, fixated, endlessly watching the numbers, documenting what value thresholds initiate an alarm and how it makes the nurses respond.

Interestingly, the heart monitor alarm does tend to elicit a fairly rapid response, which I appreciate. Seeing the urgency of the reaction as compared to the other things, however, only sparks more questions from me. Why does this one matter when the others don't? I can't stand not knowing any longer, so I do what I do.

"What does that alarm mean?" I ask after a new sound is emitted from the heart monitor.

"Oh, he's just having a brady," the nearest nurse responds.

"A brady? What's a brady? What does that mean?"

"It's short for bradycardia," she offers.

Oh, now I see. That answer is technical, accurate, and yet provides me no useful actionable information. It basically tells me nothing.

I press further into our bizarre Abott and Costello routine. "Ok, yeah, but what does that mean, what is happening?"

"His heart just stops sometimes."

The proverbial phonograph needle scratches off the record and everyone at the party pauses in the unexpected silence as that phrase just hangs in the air, uncontested, for what seems like a fortnight. "It just stops."

Come on. COME. ON. What? You can't just say that. You can't just say that to me as if it isn't a big deal. It's a ridiculous statement. His heart just stops? Why of course it does. Nope, that's not scary at all. What do you mean his heart just stops?!

My head is set to detonate at any moment, but I am calm just long enough to spit out something moderately coherent and not completely venomous.

"Wait, what? His heart just stops? That can't be right. That's not normal."

"No, it is actually. It happens a lot, particularly to preemie boys. His brain, breathing and heart connections just aren't fully developed and sometimes he stops breathing for a few seconds and his heart just stops."

At this point, I think *my* heart has stopped. Or maybe it's just pounding so hard that I just can't distinguish any space between beats. With my ticker nearly incapacitated and my mind clenched in a vice, I try to absorb and process this latest gem of information. Exhale.

"Ummm. Okay." Inhale. Now exhale again. "So, what do you do when that happens?"

"We usually just rub his back or gently tap him to get things started again."

"What?! That gets his heart restarted?"

"Yup, that's all it usually takes."

This is easily the most preposterous thing I've heard so far. I've endured a lot in the last few days, I've heard a lot of information and had to just take it in, digest it and accept it. Or at least I pretend to accept it and then check the internet or get all worked up about it, or both. But this? This new piece of information is too much.

His heart just stops sometimes, and we just rub his back? What in the world is going on here? His heart just stops? That type of phrase is usually followed by something like, "and then he died." His heart just stops sometimes. No wonder they just call it a brady, apparently to avoid internal overreactions like this one. What a name, it's inspirational really, it sounds like my favorite quarterback! What a great thing! I hope we have more of these because they sound so nice. How's your son today? Oh, he's just having a brady, nothing to see here. We're all good. No worries, his heart just stopped. Maybe he's ready for a quick small back massage and there he goes, back in business.

The absurdity confounds me. My mind can't balance the potential severity of the issue with the simplicity of the supposed remedy.

This can't be correct.

There is just no way this is correct, but more internet research confirms that indeed it is. The nurse is absolutely correct. This happens. This is happening to my son. His heart just stops and then it starts up again. I am terrified, but intrigued, and seriously, just plain weirded out.

Progress
(Day 3 in the NICU)

It's a new day, and as I arrive at the hospital and head up to the NICU, upon entering the room, I notice a new little cardboard sign with festive handwriting at the end of each of the twins' respective isolettes. On a quick glance I read that the card says "No more CRAP."

Well, that's a weird thing to say, but wouldn't that be nice if it were true, we've certainly had several doses of that lately. Maybe I should print that on a T-shirt and sell it to the masses. I'd make millions.

Upon closer inspection, I discover that I misread it the first time. The little card is a mini celebration from the nurses and it actually says "No more CPAP."

Ahh, that makes a little more sense.

The C-PAP tubes are gone. Both Eden and Roman have done so well, likely due to the steroid shots a few weeks ago, that their respiration is strong enough on its own. The CPAP is replaced with a smaller tube that supplies a faint amount of supplemental oxygen. This means there are still little pads on their face for the oxygen tubes, but it's all much smaller and less obtrusive than the C-PAP. I can see their faces quite a bit better already. It's a small but visible sign of progress and the first indication that something is going right. This is a win. I'll take it.

Good job you two. Keep fighting.

Contact

Kylene is recovering nicely and now that we've been to the NICU many times, the shock of the situation begins to ebb, and our comfort level grows. The nursing staff encourage us to get involved with the kids and their care. It's not that we weren't interacting with them in those first couple of days, but it is a little daunting to comprehend what we can do and what we can't. They're so tiny, it's hard to know.

The nurses help alleviate our uncertainty and reassure us that although the babies are small, we're not going to break them. We can change diapers, give little wipe-down baths, and hold them. We can hold them a lot if we want to, and we really want to. We want to do all the things, and frankly, we need to learn how to do all of it. These mini versions of babies are still babies after all, and someday they will need to be cared for at home without the help of the nursing staff.

With the green light from the medical staff, we dive in. We talk, we touch, we hold, we change, and we do as much as we can. We are also encouraged to spend time with them for long periods of contact referred to as skin-to-skin.

For skin-to-skin time, studies suggest that babies should be clothed in their diaper only, and mom or dad can discreetly open their shirt to allow them to lay directly on the parent's chest. This type of connection has been heralded for decades as a way for mother and baby to bond, usually in the first hour after delivery. The direct contact prompts a chemical pheromone connection which is said to improve nursing development. More recent studies indicate the connections with dad can also be rewarding; furthermore, the skin-to-skin time doesn't have to take place immediately after birth in order to be beneficial.

Regardless of which parent is involved or how long it has been since birth, the benefits of direct contact for the baby can be plentiful. First, the smells and sounds of the connecting parent become recognizable. The smell of the parent, and the sounds of their voices echoing through their chest create as sense of safety and comfort for the baby. Chemically, this connection calms the baby by reducing the levels of a stress-inducing hormone called cortisol. The baby can sense the heartbeat of the parent, which helps the baby regulate their own heartbeat. The physical proximity also transfers warmth and helps the baby to stabilize and regulate their own body temperature.

The nursing staff encourages me to wear button down shirts instead of my normal t-shirt or polo shirt to better facilitate the skin-to-skin contact. I rarely wear a button down without a white cotton undershirt, so it's not comfortable for me at first, but it's more than worth it if it helps my kids.

During my first skin-to-skin session, I feel uncertain and a little vulnerable, but it quickly proves to be enjoyable. I lay down with Roman perched on my chest, a small blanket over him and my hand over his back. My hand actually covers his entire back and more. Within a minute or two, Roman's heart rate becomes more uniform, as does his breathing, and I can tell he is getting comfortably warm. He is so small, yet so complete, and so perfect. He is an absolute wonder to behold, and to have in my arms, and spending this uninterrupted time with him is a gift.

Beyond feelings of love and connection, I didn't expect to experience any physiological effects of my own. I've read studies, however, that suggest skin-to-skin is also beneficial for the parents and can possibly lower their cortisol levels as well. Within a few minutes, much like Roman's monitored response, I can feel my heart rate slowing and I feel more calm, which is no easy feat. However skeptical I was at first, I am thoroughly convinced that this connection is working. It has a powerful effect on both of us.

Empty-Handed

(Day 4 in the NICU)

As soon as the babies were born, the insurance company dictated that Kylene is entitled to stay in the hospital two full days if she had delivered the babies traditionally but is granted three full days since she has had a c-section.

How generous, a whole extra day.

I have to shake my head at the dismissive attitude we as a society collectively hold about c-sections. I openly admit that I too was guilty of brushing this off until I witnessed it.

This is a major surgery. Routine perhaps in terms of the fact that the procedure is done regularly, but it still involves risk, injury, and recovery. The epidural, or in our case a spinal, brings risk of damage, even paralysis. Next there is a long incision right across the lower belly. Let's not forget what incision really means. My good friend, who happens to be a surgeon himself, has more than once pointed out to me the irony of surgery is that in a process meant to fix a patient, we begin by hurting them. With anesthetics, the patient should not feel it initially, but nevertheless, we are cutting them and creating an injury. In this case, I watched with my own eyes as the doctor literally took out a knife, which we give a fancy name, like scalpel, or a 10-blade, and cut through the epidermis and a few layers of subcutaneous fat. Then she mounted the table and the wrestling match with Kylene's abdominal muscles began, until the uterine wall was exposed, at which time she cut her again. With the escape hatch revealed, we remove two living humans from inside her body, and finish the extraction process by snipping the umbilical cords, effectively cutting off their only supply line of blood, oxygen, and nutrients up to that point. However common the procedure, it is still significant, invasive, and damaging. It requires skill and precision to execute, and the body needs weeks or more for healing.

Of course, all the healing doesn't have to happen in the hospital, but it is hard for me to comprehend the standard insurance company response that the c-section warrants one day more in the hospital than traditional delivery. It seems too soon. Maybe it's my geyser of worry releasing above the surface, but it just feels early. From Kylene's perspective, she doesn't need any restrictions and wants to spend every possible moment upstairs with her babies, so she is more than happy to stay as a patient to maintain her closeness to them. I want her to rest and heal; she wants to live under the same roof as her babies. We both want her to stay, but for slightly different reasons. Ultimately, we both sort of lose, as the doctors agree with insurance protocol and Kylene is discharged. This phase of three patients is over.

I gather up all her accumulated things, most of which I brought from home but am somehow surprised by how much there is. Next, I pull together the pile of gifts, cards, and snacks brought by my family, including the swirl bread. Still a few slices left, which I have my eye on.

Having assembled all our gear, we make a last trip upstairs to see the kids and say goodnight for the day. I have been conducting this ritual and a sendoff for myself since the first day, but right now is Kylene's first encounter with the weight of this reality. We are leaving. More specifically, she is leaving, and the babies are not. Up until right now, even though her patient room was several floors down, she was always in the building, living in the same house, so to speak. Her patient discharge ends that proximity. In the next few minutes, we will leave the room, and then leave the building, and leave our precious babies behind. The mere thought of this truth is agony, and the emotional stormfront rolls in quickly. The emotional difficulty of leaving them surprises Kylene, and though I expected some struggles, it's worse than I feared. Her tears flow silently again and though they eventually subside, they remain just beneath the surface, threatening to resume as we walk out the door, down the hallway, and onto the elevator.

The orderly pushes her discharge wheelchair to the front doors of the hospital, while I go and fetch the car from the parking structure. When I return a few minutes later, I quietly load her stuff inside as she gets in the passenger seat. The emptiness I felt driving home the first night returns, only this time it's different. For me it's better because she is with me, but at the same time it is worse because that means she isn't with them. For her, there could be nothing worse than this situation. This is wrong. This isn't how it's supposed to be. Our babies are supposed to be with us, there are supposed to be balloons on the mailbox, and we are supposed to be embarking on the first sleepless night at home with crying babies. It should be a day of celebration and excitement. Instead, aside from some sniffling from the passenger seat, the car is silent as we drive home empty-handed, wallowing in our misery.

Head and Heart Trauma
(Day 5 in the NICU)

After our first night home alone, we are eager to get back into the NICU to see the kids. Coming in today feels different, a new era of sorts. Kylene isn't a patient anymore, and while she's still got some healing to do, she is fully immersed in mom mode. I don't know how she already knows what to do, but she does. Is this purely maternal instinct, or does she have some sort of elaborate practice facility hidden at home in our basement? Regardless, she's already really good at all aspects of baby care. They are lucky to have her.

At some point during the day, the nurses notice that Eden's IV has come out. I don't know how or what happened. It may have been accidentally snagged or she may have pulled it out as she flailed around in her isolette. Hats come off, they somehow manage to lose a sock, monitor sensors come unstuck, and I guess sometimes the IV comes out. It's not a big deal and it's nobody's fault, but since the IV is supplying medicine and her nutrient load, someone has to put in a new IV. This, unfortunately, requires poking a needle into my baby girl's hand or arm.

If you're a parent and you've had an infant or toddler who needs to get shots, you know where I'm coming from. You go to the doctor and eventually the dreaded moment arrives. The big needle comes out and they stab it right in the meatiest part of your baby's arm or thigh. Watching the poke is crushing, but witnessing the response is worse. The kid usually opens their mouth in a moment of silent anguish, that brief fragment of time in which they display the look of shock, horror, and clear betrayal. Afterward comes the crying, a pained wail of misery that is usually able to be quelled within a few moments.

If you've lived through infant shots, you might have a sense of some fraction of this feeling, but the IV is a whole other level. Eden weighs three pounds. Her head is just larger than a tennis ball. She is tiny, skinny and she has very tiny veins, which makes this IV task difficult to perform and very difficult for dad to watch.

It's time. The young nurse comes over with the fresh IV kit, lays out the line and the needle, and wipes Eden's tiny arm with the alcohol pad to prevent infection. I steel myself to watch my daughter endure pain and try to touch her and talk to her through the moment. The poke happens, her face sours from pain and she lets out a high-pitched cry. My blood pressure rises and my heart breaks. If you've heard a newborn cry, you know the sound of those short, repetitive wails. Preemie cries are more muted, but even more gut-wrenching.

"It's ok, it's all done," I quietly reassure her, relieved that it's over.

The nurse comments, "Oh shoot, it didn't work."

"What do you mean it didn't work?" I wasn't prepared for this not working.

"I must have missed the vein," she casually quips, "they're so tiny, it's hard sometimes. I'll have to do it again." Her words are very matter of fact and seemingly unconcerned, as if she just forgot to file a form in the right folder.

"No big deal, I'll just do it again."

I choose not to say much, a rare choice for me, but my mind is racing.

Do what again? Stab my helpless three-pound infant with a needle? Because you missed? You missed!? So now she and I have to do this again? This may be a casual mistake to you, but my preemie girl's well-being is at stake here. Not to mention my fragmented mind.

"Here we go, let's try this again on the other hand this time and…oh, that didn't work either."

You missed again? Again!?

My anger builds, roiling and threatening to boil over. I can feel it coming; this is not going to be good. Then, on her third try, the nurse misses again. Three swings, three strikes, you're out.

"You know, sometimes I can't get this right," she explains.

This has got to be the worst explanation in the history of the universe.

She continues, "I think we should have Nancy do it, she's the best at putting in the IVs."

My heart has been torn asunder as my frustration and anger escalate into a fuming rage.

What do you MEAN, you sometimes don't get it?! Isn't this your job? Aren't you supposed to be good at this? If you can't do it, why did you even start? Was it just to practice, and fail three times, THREE TIMES, on my poor, helpless daughter?

"Maybe Nancy should have just done it in the first place, so we can get it done right on the first try and not have to poke Eden an extra three times."

Oh no. That part happened out loud.

The contempt in my voice is sharp and probably unfair, but I don't care. My daughter is hurt, I am hurt, and I am not thinking about anyone else. Not in this moment, not right now. I want the best possible care for my baby, and I don't care if I'm being impolite. I am her advocate, and I will demand better. Loudly and, it turns out, rudely, if necessary. If she liked me before, I'm guessing the nurse doesn't like me now. I don't blame her, but I don't care. I'm done with her.

Nancy comes over and examines the battlefield that is Eden's hands and arms. She gently heats Eden's arm with a warm blanket in an effort to warm up and expand the veins for better access. Satisfied that she has a new target for a successful campaign, she pokes Eden again. She misses too. Strike four.

I am incensed. No, that doesn't really even begin to describe it. I'm at a complete loss. The most visceral emotional pain sears through every fiber of my being, and my seething anger threatens to engulf me and anyone in my general vicinity.

What in the world is going on?

(Insert unspoken expletives.)

Why can't anyone do their job here?

I can't imagine how this could possibly get any worse.

Nancy offers, "You know, the best place to do infant IVs is actually in the head. We'll just do that and I'm sure it will work."

Welp. I was wrong. This is worse. This is markedly worse. I instantly loath this idea. We already have an oxygen tube in her nose, a pulse-ox cuff on her foot, occasional ultraviolet glow lights, a heart monitor, and countless other devices hooked to my three-pound daughter. Now we are going to put a needle in her *head*?

Alert the village in the valley below, the concrete face of the dam is cracking, water is seeping through the fissures, the damage is irreparable, and the remnants unsalvageable. Collapse is imminent.

The nurses clip and shave a small spot of hair on Eden's head and successfully get the IV inserted on the first try. Well, it's actually the fifth try, but the first try on the head. They quickly make up another little celebration card exclaiming "First haircut!"

I understand they are doing their best, but I am uninterested in the forced fanfare. I am not amused. I am not in the mood to be celebrating; in fact, it makes me more upset. I am broken and devastated. I'm mad at the nurses, yes, but underneath I am upset with myself. I am failing. I am failing my daughter, and she is suffering. Her suffering delivers me repeated doses of anger, guilt and frustration at my futility and inability to help her. I am not in control.

Nancy seems to have forgiven my insensitivity and she notices I am sinking deeper into my pit of despair. In an act of grace, she makes a compassionate suggestion,

"I think we should get you set up for a skin-to-skin session with Eden. I think you both could use it right now."

I'm not thinking clearly at all right now, but I think she's right. I do need something instead of just standing here fuming. Right now, I probably need some skin-to-skin much more than Eden. I get a reclining chair into position, lay back, unbutton my shirt, and the nurse carefully hands Eden to me. I place her on my chest and then cover us with a small blanket.

Eden nestles into me, and her breathing and heart rate settle as she marinates in my heartbeat, my breathing, and my body heat. I close my eyes and gently wrap my hands around her tiny body, holding her, protecting her, and wishing away the pain. I exhale deeply, my heart still stained with profound sadness. But now there is a glimmer of hope rising. Slowly my blood pressure falls, the tension releases ever so slightly, and the frayed nerves begin to heal.

Words my mom had spoken a day or two earlier echo in my frazzled mind. "You will remember this, but they won't." She meant the whole ordeal, not just this past hour of fresh suffering, but the reminder of her sage words actually helps right now, more than I expected. I know she's right. I know it is true, and Eden will not remember this pain. Their physical pain and my feelings of frustration and anger will not imprint into their memories. It will not shape or scar them. But for me, on the other hand, this darkness, this valley of abject helplessness, my failure to protect my daughter… it will all be indelibly etched into my mind. These painful memories will be with me forever, but they will also be mixed with this feeling of peace and love I feel as I hold her to my chest. She will never remember these NICU days. I will never forget.

Gavage

We've graduated out of needing the CPAP and now the IV is out too. On purpose this time. These are incredible points of progress, but now a new visible oddity is featured. In the very corner of their mouths is a small, clear plastic tube. Even though it is thin in diameter and not nearly as intrusive as the CPAP hose, it still feels out of place and unnatural and seeing it makes me a little bit sad.

The tube is for gavage feeding. It bypasses their need to swallow and instead deposits the food, or in this case milk or formula, directly into their stomachs. Oral receipt of nutrition, even if with a tube, is still progress beyond the IV and is something to be happy about. It means the stomach enzymes and other digestive mechanisms are functionally ready, but the suck-swallow-breathe reflex still needs time to develop. They still can't take a bottle, but that should be coming soon and that additional progress on the horizon is comforting.

What is less comforting for me is how the staff puts in the tube. I've watched it happen several times. From what I can surmise, the basic process seems to be "measuring" the right length of the tube by laying it on the baby's body, estimating where the stomach is (from the outside mind you) then marking the tube and inserting it. Granted, they use a little more care and are clearly experienced, but still, this method seems filled with opportunities for mishap.

As they work on Roman, I wonder aloud, "What if you perforate his esophagus, or his stomach with that tube?"

"Oh, that won't happen, I've done this hundreds of times," replies the self-assured nurse.

In my mind though, it *could* happen, so as honest and good natured as his response is, these assurances do not make me feel any less anxious.

Perhaps I should explain further. This isn't about distrust of the medical staff, at least not entirely, and it's not even a tendency toward pessimism, though I've been accused of that too. I just look at things in life with what I feel is a lens of realism, and that often leads me down the path of exploring the "what if."

I'll admit, I am also tainted by my work in forensic engineering. I don't investigate buildings that are doing fine, I only get involved when things go wrong, and failures occur. It's analogous to the worship song lyric I sang one Sunday in church that says, "Only the sick need a physician." Only the buildings with problems need someone like me. That makes sense.

This also means the majority of my experience is with buildings that have suffered an acute event or are experiencing a systemic ongoing failure. My job is to identify the failure mechanism of what went wrong and why. Spending so much time figuring out what is wrong naturally leads me to try and predict what else *could* go wrong before it even happens. In my world, every building has a problem, or eventually will, and I can probably tell you what it will be.

There's the rub; everything in the world has risks and probabilities surrounding it, and I can't help but see the possible chain of events leading to calamity: if this happens, then this might happen, and then this could happen as a result. That's how my job has taught me to think, and now it colors all aspects of my life.

Fortunately, this way of looking at the world hasn't turned me into a nervous person, or even someone who worries a lot. It does, however, make me think through things more thoroughly than most. Whether consciously or not, I strategically review the possible outcomes to help me prepare, both mentally and physically, for what might happen next.

When I'm with my babies in the NICU, I see all the potential things that could go wrong with everything—the gavage tube, with the heart monitor, or with the nursing staff protocols—and then I ask questions, and conduct my own research to understand the technical aspects of what is happening, what the equipment means and how it works, and what to expect so that I can mentally prepare for the next challenge. The insights I gain from this process somewhat satisfy my technical curiosity but are at best a weak balm for my worried soul.

When it's a building failure that I suspect might happen, if my prediction is right, the concrete cracks or the wood roof truss member fractures, and we have a big mess to clean up. I can design the repairs. When it's my three-pound infant with the potential for something going wrong, life hangs in the balance.

So, I worry. In fact, I deftly maintain various tiers of worry. Circling back to today's worry du jour: the gavage tube. I know Roman needs the tube for his nutrition and I'm glad to be done with the IV and advanced to this next phase, but still, there's worry. What if he can't develop further and learn the next phase? What if they mess it up and hurt his throat or stomach? There are even whispers of the remote possibility of him eventually going home while still needing gavage feeding. Going home sounds great, but gavage at home means I would have to learn to insert the tube. Not impossible, but this is not an option I'm interested in considering quite yet. I have enough concerns with the experienced staff inserting the tube, and I certainly don't want to be responsible for doing it myself.

For now, we're not at home. We're still in the NICU, and despite my concerns, the tube is already in, he's taking the feeding, and his stomach is handling it fine. So far, so good. To the nurse's credit, there is no disaster. They do seem to be pretty good at putting it in. That will just have to be good enough for now and I'll have to live with it, not being in control. Not that I have much of a choice anyway.

Wimpy White Boy

(Day 6 in the NICU)

It has been several days now and Roman is a little down on weight. At birth he weighed in at 3 pounds 7 ounces but has lost a few ounces and is down to 3 pounds and 4 ounces. Evidently that's normal, losing weight after birth, but when you start at a measly three pounds, losing three ounces is more of a big deal. Eden is down a little too, but since Roman started smaller, he's the focus and the greater cause for concern.

He needs to put on weight and that's not so easy. He isn't a teenager who we can stuff with white bread or macaroni and cheese for a carb load. He is a tiny human, who weighs less than an obnoxiously large burrito at some Mexican eatery. At a good feeding, he can maybe consume up to one ounce. One ounce! A standard water bottle is 8 to 12 ounces. The volume of one ounce of milk or formula is 30 mL equivalent to just about two tablespoons. Tablespoons. For you and me, that's an ingredient, maybe even the seasoning. For Roman, it's an entire meal. It takes time to gain an ounce, and he needs to gain many ounces and eventually pounds. In a perfect world, he would weigh twice as much as he does. Imagine trying to double your weight.

As we discuss what is already a stressful topic, a few nurses are quick to cite some seemingly nebulous pile of statistics. I get the gist of their point pretty quickly. To me, they are trying to explain away his predicament.

"White boys don't fare as well in the NICU."

"White boys just don't fight as hard."

"White boys are slow to grow and thrive."

"White boys don't survive as often."

These statements are actually made out loud. These stanzas of discouragement culminate in the declaration that that's just how it is, that he's likely going to struggle, simply because he's a "wimpy white boy." A chorus of other nurses echoes the sentiment. Yup. Wimpy white boy. Just a wimpy white boy. The table is set with built-in excuses as they say the phrase out loud over and over.

My ire is inflamed, and my inner monologue is whipped into a frothing fervor once again. My muted voice is screaming.

What in the world is this? This is absolute garbage they're spewing. Wimpy white boy? Are you kidding me?

Their comments might be based on years of on-the-job observations or even some study validating gender or ethnicity-based patterns among NICU babies, but none of that really matters to me. Regardless of the reason, regardless of whether their words were meant to sting or they are just the result of idle tactlessness, I hate what I feel is a carelessly applied label: Wimpy white boy. My blood pressure rises further.

Who do you think you are? Why would you say that to me? Why would you say that, ever? Is that supposed to be helpful? Is this meant to encourage the supposed strength of my daughter but at the expense of my son? Is that what this has come to? Is this meant to meter expectations, or does it just help to breed complacency amongst the staff? Are you giving up on him? It feels like you are. Or maybe this is just a way to erode hope?

I'm fuming.

I don't need my expectations to be tempered, I don't need excuses based on some other babies, I need help. I need solutions. I need results. I need him to gain weight. There is no excuse for you so casually dismissing my son. My son! This is MY son. I don't care what you're used to seeing. I don't care what you think. He isn't some data point on your chart. He isn't just another baby in a long line of babies coming in and out of here. He is my son. He's laying right there, with all the wires and monitors and the machines and that tube sticking out the corner of his mouth. And he's...

I look down to inform the details of my silent tantrum and notice he's smiling. Roman is smiling. A little sideways smirk with his eyes closed, somehow, he's reminding me it's going to be okay. He doesn't know the issue, and he's completely at ease. I am not at ease. But this little guy has done just enough to disarm me, momentarily at least, and I thank God for the gift smiling in front of me.

I've never been the model of restraint and I don't know which, if any, of my angry thoughts escaped my mouth as audible words. I'm fairly certain I didn't say anything out loud, but I definitely thought about plenty of things I wanted to say, and I suspect I displayed my disdain with my poorly hidden facial expressions. Whatever I did or said, I made it clear I didn't want to hear that again. Don't say "wimpy white boy" about my son. Ever again.

I'm not making friends here, but honestly, that's not my priority. My kids are all that matter.

Reunited

(Day 7 in the NICU)

Today as we arrive at the hospital and enter the NICU, we are surprised to learn that they moved one of the babies. The other child separating our two was discharged to a different section of the hospital, freeing up the real estate in the crowded room so that Roman and Eden can be next to each other. This is a nice surprise for us, and while it likely makes no difference to either of the twins, it provides many positive benefits for us as parents. The logistics of our presence with them is improved. I can sit in one place and be next to both of them. We can sit together and be with both of them. This may sound silly and unimportant, but it is huge. The new arrangement lifts our spirits.

By far the biggest benefit is that it allows each of us to take a turn holding both babies at the same time. It is one of those things we didn't know we were missing until we got to do it for the first time, and then doing so thrust the reality of twins directly into the spotlight. I have two babies and I'm holding them both right now, together. My hands are full, my heart is full, and my life is full of blessings. In these two tiny bundles there is so much life and surrounding them is so much love. I'll never forget this moment, holding them both. Together. Reunited. They have lived their entire life in the same space and have rarely even been in different rooms. They were one station apart and that was too far. This proximity feels different, it feels right. It feels better.

Holding them next to each other, I also get to see them respond to each other. Perched in my arms on a pillow on my lap, I pull them right next to each other, touching. Eden wriggles her nose and shies away, perhaps unready to share quarters again, but Roman noticeably smiles. They probably have no clue what's going on, but I pretend they do, and it makes me happy.

Part VIII – Learning

Under Pressure

(Day 8 in the NICU)

Everything in life has changed so much in the last few days. Things that were once so important are no longer relevant, and two humans whom I had previously never laid eyes on now occupy my mind constantly. When I'm not with my kids, I miss them, I want to see them, and I want to know if they are okay. When I'm with them and allow myself to take a breath to just be present in the moment with them, I find myself mesmerized. I'm still often frustrated and worried, but the joy and wonder of staring at my son and touching his head or talking to my daughter and holding her hand have me transfixed, and the power of those feelings is starting to take the edge off of my reactions and softening my hardened exterior.

I'm also starting to absorb what I've been hearing from staff and seeing how they interact with my kids as compared to the other kids in the NICU. It is not a competition, and we all want every single kid in here to win and go home to their family, but I'm beginning to notice that both Eden and Roman are actually doing comparatively well. Although some of their progress is sullied by small steps of regression, their overall trajectories are positive. The nurses have even begun to categorize our two as "growers and feeders." Though I did not appreciate the other label some nurses put on Roman, this label is a good thing. In fact, it's the best label in the NICU, because "grower and feeder" really means there is nothing fundamentally wrong with them, and they just need time to develop. They need to complete on the outside what most babies finish doing on the inside.

All they need is time, but how much time? Since the babies arrived at the NICU, we've been given an oft-quoted rule of thumb to help set our general expectations: They'll be here until their due date. For us, that is nine weeks to reach their full gestational age. That math makes plenty of sense, but that calendar date is disheartening. Nine weeks of this? It's early December now, that projects out to February. That is a really long time but as daunting as that assignment feels, it is still encouraging to hear the conversation shift to discuss *when* they will go home with no more scary notions of *if* they'll go home.

Now there are whispers discharging them not in nine weeks, but maybe more like five weeks since they seem to be doing so well. We are not in a rush, and we want them to be ready, but this possibility is another glimmer of hope.

With this new vector, there is palpable relief. We have a plan, we have some new and improved expectations, and I think the kids are going to be okay. The decompression is not immediate, but it's there, and I think we are both starting to feel a slow leak, gradually allowing the dangerously high levels of pressure to bleed off. I don't notice any changes in my own behavior, but while talking to one of the nurses, I make a wisecrack, laced with playful sarcasm. Nothing out of the ordinary for me, at least under normal conditions. I even laugh at my own attempt at humor as she laughs too. Then she stops and says something I didn't expect,

"It's good to see you smile, Ross."

I counter that, a little defensively, "What do you mean?"

"You've been in crisis mode for days, and I think you're finally starting to act like yourself again."

Her comment isn't an accusation so much as an observation, and an astute one since I suspect she's probably right. Even though she only met me a week ago, she can see a change in me as I start to relax back into my usual self. She has probably seen the whole process before with other parents. One thing is for certain though. I *have* been in crisis mode like she said. I've been surviving a crisis I didn't create and one that I can't contain. It has affected me so personally and so profoundly that I have been thrown off axis for these past few days and I have been spiraling out of control. This realization that we might be just a few short weeks from bringing our babies home has righted me and given me the hope I needed. Now that I believe they're going to be okay, I might just be okay too.

Peripheral Vision

Though I've come to realize that Roman and Eden are on the right trajectory, I'm also painfully aware that not every baby in this room is so lucky. I've been here for days, for many hours at a time, and as captivating as my children are, I still have to get up and walk around a little every now and again. When I leave their bedsides, sometimes I leave the room for a few minutes for a mental break, but usually I just pace around the room or I go over and look out the window — anything, really, to stretch my legs.

During my countless laps around the room, I've learned to recognize most of the other babies, and their names are displayed on their isolettes for me to learn and remember. From repetition comes familiarity, and from that comes investment. I care. I don't know each baby's whole story, and privacy regulations don't allow the nurses to tell me medical details, but I've gathered bits and pieces over time, such that I've begun to surmise various things.

One little guy has a hole in his heart and needs surgery. But first he must grow big enough to be stable enough for surgery, but he doesn't grow very fast because of his heart. It's a classic Catch-22 scenario with the most dire of potential outcomes.

That one across the room is huge by NICU standards, I estimate he's at least eight pounds, a giant amongst his preemie peers, but something isn't developing right. Again, I don't know the details, but I can see he is still hooked up to all the equipment, even more than we started with.

These two babies and several of the others have serious struggles ahead; with significant, critical issues they must overcome. I'm thankful my kids don't carry the same burdens; there is nothing fundamentally wrong with them, and they just need more time.

As this truth sinks in, I am grateful, but a new wave of feelings starts to breach the horizon. The sensation comes on gradually, like how a parade float slowly starts to glide into view: an unexpected, yet unmistakable sensation of guilt. Guilt for how I've been feeling and thinking. Not because my feelings weren't genuine or because all the fears and distress weren't warranted, but because it could have been much worse. I've been pretty busy feeling sorry for myself, my heart hurting for my kids' situation and the many departures from my dreams and expectations. Now I'm seeing that they have nearly the best prognosis possible, at least for kids who land here in this place. I am simultaneously thrilled that my kids are headed toward health and heartbroken that other parents and their kids aren't as fortunate. My sense of relief stands, but guilt infiltrates as my peripheral vision clears and I can start to see and feel for the other families around us.

Learning the Ropes

We have eclipsed a week here in the NICU and already it has become less daunting and more of a second home for us. I guess it's fitting really, since the twins haven't left the room, this sort of is their current home. And, since we haven't missed a day being at their sides, it has become where we spend a lot of our time.

A new set of rhythms has emerged in our daily routine. For me, nights are still very similar to my pre-children schedule. I go to sleep and then I wake up in the morning. But, on the other side of the bed, things have changed. Every night in the middle of the night, Kylene wakes up to call the NICU night nurse.

On that first emotional night when we left and I took Kylene home, the charge nurse gave us a number we could call and assured us it would be answered all night long. They understood about the separation difficulty and genuinely encouraged us to call anytime. I don't know how many people actually choose to call, but Kylene does. She calls every night around the same time to check on them, to get a report on their status from the nurse, and to hear that everything is fine. We can't be *there*, they can't be *here*, so she calls. Every night.

So far, the night reports have all been positive, but each includes enough specific details that we believe they are authentic. At least Kylene thinks so, because she's the only one who hears them, and she tells me all about the reports the next morning when I wake up. I appreciate her updates, I just don't choose to call myself. It's not that I don't care, or that I don't worry. I do, I worry a lot and I think about the kids constantly, about everything. But I've also had to relinquish some control. Total control actually, which is incredibly difficult for me. I have to acknowledge that as much as I want to, I can't solve this problem. I can ask questions and research to understand the issues, but I can't fix them.

I help the kids however I can, with my presence in the room by their isolette, or my skin contact, or my vocal advocacy in certain moments, but I am not a neonatologist and I'm not God. I have to trust that God has a plan for my kids, and part of that plan is these doctors and nurses being in this hospital to help my kids. I believe that, and I trust that. I *have* to trust that, because otherwise I will go completely crazy.

With that all stated, I'm still glad Kylene calls every night, and if she didn't, I probably would. Who am I kidding, I definitely would, because I would need to know all the information. Luckily, I have her motherly instincts fueling the information gathering for me, so I don't need to duplicate her efforts. So, every night, I sleep, and she calls.

Every morning, we get up and get ready for the day and then load into my truck for the journey to the hospital together. Kylene is still restricted from driving due to her c-section incision, so she needs me to chauffeur her around for a week or two. I drive her to the hospital and drop her off with her purse, a sack lunch, her pumping gear, various snacks, and clean baby clothes for the kids. She goes upstairs and spends the entire day in the NICU with the kids.

Meanwhile, I reluctantly go to work. I desperately want to be there in the NICU too, but we have decided that I should save my limited time off for when the babies are home and all three of them will need my help the most.

For now, Kylene has endless help available to her in the NICU, but she doesn't use it much. Kylene dresses them, changes diapers, gives sponge baths, and, as bottle feedings increase in size and frequency, Kylene does most of that too. The nurses are happy to teach her the subtle differences between caring for preemies versus full-term babies, and they encourage all the parents to start learning the care routine. Even so, I suspect Kylene does more than most. She does all the work. Of course there is medical care that she's not qualified to perform, but by choice, the rest of the care is on her docket. Not because the nursing care is inadequate, but because she wants to do it; she feels she *needs* to do it, because she is their mom.

Every evening after work, I drive straight to the hospital, select the most efficiently proximate parking spot available to minimize my walking distance, and expertly navigate my way in to see my family. When I arrive, Kylene is dutifully by the side of one of the kids and provides detailed status update reports. Most days, the news is of positive progression for each, but sometimes there are negative regressions, and even though these are usually temporary, I still bristle with renewed concern every time one of them gets a less than perfect report card.

Whether the reports are good or bad, these are the best few hours of my day. This is my time to be where I want to be. I spend time with each of them, talking to them, touching their hands and heads, holding them, and generally feasting my eyes on everything they do. I pay attention to how their dimensions and measurements change every day; their cheeks are a little fuller, the readings on the monitor screens are more stable, and the feedings a little larger. Conversely, while their physical markers continuously change, their personalities are remarkably consistent and recognizable. Eden and Roman are clearly very different from each other, but each of them have developed a persona that stays the same from one day to the next.

Eden is stoic and quiet. She doesn't complain much unless something is specifically not to her liking, and when said issue is resolved, she quickly resumes her posture of indifference. She seems irritated by the various noises of the room and just pulls her hat down over her ears a little more and turns the other way. I know that sounds crazy — she's only days old and has no control over her body or limbs - yet it seems she does this deliberately as it happens all the time.

Roman is more expressive than his sister, quick with a smirk or smile, but equally quick to frown, or cry if his expectations of ideal life conditions aren't met one hundred percent. He makes us laugh a lot at his seemingly endless kaleidoscope of emotions. Neither is better than the other, they are just different, each remarkably their own person, even at just a few days old. They are each a perfect gift of life and are already uniquely themselves.

They also look more like babies. When they were first born, they were so skinny and there was so much equipment around them. They were just lying in the isolettes in their diapers. and the visual was pretty foreign. It was not what I envisioned for a newborn baby. It felt almost alien. That sounds harsh but it's how I felt, and that unexpected image accented the pain and worry of those first few hours.

They are still tiny and still thin, but they look more like babies now. Certainly, the slight weight gain and improved skin coloration are a big part of this, but I think the clothes help a lot too. The preemie clothes are still way too big for them, but Kylene has them dressed anyway, the clothes seem to accentuate their personalities. It also feels better to see them wearing *their* clothes and holding them with *their* blankets. It's subtle, and probably a bit silly, but it still feels better. I'll take what I can get.

It also feels good to be taking care of our kids. Granted, Kylene does the majority of the work, but she's still on my team, so I'm decreeing that we'll collectively take the credit. She's learning, we're learning, and we're getting comfortable. Afterall, at some point, who knows how long from now — we're going to need to be doing all of this by ourselves at home. With so many medical aspects still in the mix, right now, that seems like a daunting proposition. But it's coming, and we're learning the ropes to prepare for the eventuality that we hope and pray comes soon.

Presence

(Day 9 in the NICU)

The progress for Roman and Eden remains remarkably positive and almost every day they advance further than we expected. Every gain feels like a win. Of course, this is not a competition and I want every kid to race out of this hospital as quickly as possible. No kid, no parent, no grandparent, no one, should have to endure even a moment of this.

With all that fine print stated for context and humility, it still feels like we are winning. It seems like our kids are outpacing nearly everyone else in the NICU. When it comes to the other kids in the "growers and feeders" group, our twins are moving faster. Everything is the same between the patients, except for one factor: we are here. We are *always* here, at least one of us, and I think it is making a difference.

No one spends more time with our babies than Kylene and me. She is here all day and I come late afternoon to join her. We are here, talking to the kids, touching their hands, feet, and faces, smiling at them, being attentive, encouraging, celebrating, and fighting for and alongside them.

We are simply present. This is our existence. There are other kids who rarely have visitors and one baby for whom I have never seen anyone. His parents are from East Jordan, a city more than two-and-a-half hours away by car. It's impossible for them to be here. We live nearby, we don't have other kids to deal with at home, we *can* be here, and so we *are* here. Every. Single. Day.

I am increasingly confident that our being here matters, that somehow our consistency of presence and frequency of interaction has a direct positive impact on Eden and Roman's growth and progress. I don't mean for it to sound like I'm congratulating myself on winning a nonexistent NICU parent competition, but let's face it, this kind of thinking fits my profile: perfectionist, problem solver, overachiever… maybe even a robot in the sense that I am singularly focused and won't quit until we see results. It checks the boxes of all these flaws that I know I have. Despite sounding so reprehensible, I'm unequivocally convinced of my position: being here matters, and it's the reason our babies are outpacing so many of their peers.

This realization fills me with gratitude that we can be here. The babies whose families are loving them and worrying about them from a distance seem to be fighting their battles alone. But they are not actually alone, not if you pay close attention. Even though they have thoroughly demanding job duties, the stress of multiple babies to care for, and the burden of dealing with unreasonable crisis-laden parents, (some who are engineers), the NICU nurses find time to do even more for these babies.

The nurses hold them, and talk to them, and smile at them. This is beyond their assignment or duty. This is compassion and love exemplified. I see it firsthand, how the NICU nurses step into the void when parents can't be here. As I hold a conversation with her, I watch one nurse scoop up and cuddle a baby as if it is her own daughter. You would never suspect otherwise, save for the uniform she wears and her obvious medical knowledge. She interacts with the baby for many minutes and then she sheepishly scolds herself in a moment of admission to me.

"We're not supposed to kiss them…" she confesses.

It's clear she understands why, from germs, and other preventative sanitary precautions, but her admission implies she still wants to and maybe even has done so accidentally a few times. She loves this baby, and that baby over there, and likely mine too, though they are rarely not being hovered over by a parent. Maybe it's not quite the same as a mother or father's love, but it isn't just transactional. It is genuine, spontaneous, and impactful. She doesn't kiss the baby, but she would if she could, and I'm convinced the baby knows that. The baby knows that someone who cares deeply is holding her and is fighting for her in this moment. Perhaps all the kids in here have a shot at winning after all.

A Week Off

Decades of research and accumulated data in the neonatology field have yielded a well-documented medical timeline of how infant development works. We know when the eyes develop, when the lungs can support respiration, and when the cranial plates fuse.

Even though most of the growing and feeding that Roman and Eden are doing right now was supposed to happen in utero, the medical team now keeps careful track of all the happenings here on the outside. They know what is supposed to happen and when, but preemie development can also be a little bit unpredictable. Each baby is on their own path, and those paths can be somehow simultaneously slow and fast, regimented, and free flowing. Despite these differences in progress from one baby to the next, there are clear signposts along the way that signal improvement. For example, when it came to oxygen and C-PAP, the item was just disconnected when they didn't need it anymore. When their bilirubin levels got to where they were supposed to be, the phototherapy treatments ended. No checking of the calendar, no resistance, just move on and move up.

In contrast, when it comes time to progress from IV nutrition to gavage, or to introduce bottle feeding, the medical team also uses the babies' ages, combined with other physical signs and markers, to determine when they are ready for each new step. Knowing this, I pay close attention to the calendar, counting down the days to each prospective new milestone. Based on her progress and their age, I think Eden is ready and Roman is within a day of being ready to try the bottle, but when I ask a nurse about this, she won't let us try.

"They're not old enough. They need to be 32 weeks," the nurse explains.

"But they are 32 weeks," I respond, a little confused.

"You shouldn't rush them, they can't bottle feed until 32 weeks, they're not ready yet," she replies.

"If they aren't ready, I'm fine waiting, but based on the other nurses, and what I'm seeing, I think they're ready."

"Well, they are not allowed to try until 32 weeks."

"They are 32 weeks!" I'm growing more and more irate with this conversation.

The back and forth continues for a few more rounds until the source of the problem is revealed.

"I think you're mistaken," she says. "The chart says they are 31 weeks."

"They were born at 30 weeks and 6 days, and we've been here over a week. They are 32 weeks."

"The chart says they were born at 29 weeks, 6 days. You're a week ahead."

"Your chart is wrong. You're a week behind. Who filled out this chart?" I ask, my voice growing more frustrated.

"Doctor So-and-So (obviously not her real name), she's a resident."

I've learned to take the fight to the source. I know when my kids were born. Kylene knows when they were born. Our OB knows when they were born. Even our pediatrician, who has only seen them once, knows when they were born. When your kids are born nine weeks early, you know the numbers. You absolutely know the numbers. It was 30 weeks and 6 days. I'm positive.

After tracking down the resident and then going to the charge nurse and various other iterations of the same circular argument, we finally find someone who either just believes us, has found some way to confirm what we are saying, or just wants me to stop bothering them. They acknowledge that we are right. I don't know which factor weighed most heavily, but we have prevailed, and the chart is corrected.

This mistake cost my kids at least a day of learning to bottle feed, maybe two. Had we not pushed back, it would have cost them over a week. Does this change the course of history? Will this affect what college they get into? No, probably not (but it could!) but I don't have that long view in mind yet. We are here fighting their battles by minute-by-minute and hour-by-hour. When it comes to their growth and development, every moment, and every ounce counts and this could have cost us a WEEK. In our present reality, this constitutes a colossal mistake. A whole week off.

With today's frustration resolved, I go back to the charge nurse and request — or rather demand — that the resident who made the charting error no longer work on my kids. If I can't rely on her to get that critical detail recorded correctly, then I'm not interested in her capabilities being applied in other more crucial functions. The charge nurse gives me no pushback or grief over the request and makes a note of it. I have only the slightest twinge of remorse, as there could be some repercussions for the resident. I don't want her fired or anything, but I definitely don't want her around the Smith isolettes. I'm fighting for my kids and doing what I think is best for them.

Doctor, Doctor

Our daily family routine has been established, I am comfortable with the equipment, and now we are starting to understand how the medical team oversees our care. There is a team of thirteen neonatologist doctors, and instead of dividing the population and monitoring their own grouping of patients, all the doctors monitor all the patients. The group meets every morning to discuss status and treatment which is encouraging because a veritable brain trust is contemplating everything that is happening and keeping my kids under the best care plan. On the flip side, this means we see a different rounding doctor each day. They come around the same time, they all have the charts, and they know the cases on account of the meetings, but we as parents don't have daily continuity of messaging and aren't developing a comfort level through a relationship with any one doctor.

The nursing rotation is more consistent, and we are quick to identify our favorites and admittedly the ones we don't prefer. They all know the job and seem safe, but some have a different personal touch, more heartwarming than the others.

Outside our realm of familiarity, we also perceive how the greater hospital operations work as we see, and more specifically we hear, hints all day. On top of the symphony of alarms, the hospital public address speakers add another level of noise as pages are announced every few minutes.

"Dr Anderson, please dial extension 4223."

"Code blue on floor three, code blue on floor three."

"Dr. Johnson, please come to room 253, Dr. Johnson, room 253."

The additional disruptions are annoying, especially in a space already filled with alarms, and beeping monitors, and interruptions, and stress, but the information is understandably necessary, important, and simply part of a functioning hospital. And, if you pay close enough attention, the intercom pages bring an occasional bit of unintentional comic relief.

One of the neonatologist's last name is Doctor. You've got that right. Dr. Doctor. So naturally, when he is paged, it elicits immature smirks from me. Every time.

"Dr. Doctor, please dial 1324. Dr. Doctor, 1324."

Somewhere 80s sensation Robert Palmer is predicting the doctor will soon be musically diagnosing a "bad case of loving you." Hilarious. I had a graduate assistant in my materials science engineering class, MSE250 at Michigan, whose last name was Engineer. That coincidence was bad enough. Mehernosh Engineer, the engineer. But we engineers don't adorn our names with the prefacing title of Engineer. *Maybe we should.* Polymath Engineer Smith. It has a certain ring to it. Anyway, poor Dr. Doctor, what a journey through medical school he must have had. You know he gets asked daily if that is his real name. He must. (I know I would ask.) He's probably an incredible doctor. I've even met him a couple of times, and he seems great, but the name is everything, and I love it.

Every time his name is called over the PA, I hear it and I smile. Then like Pavlov's dog, I finish the song lyric, out loud, to whoever is within earshot. I kind of have to, because if I can't enjoy this simple thing, then I'm worse off than I thought.

"Dr. Doctor..."

"...gimme the news."

The Milk Maven

Despite all the tasks we are learning, there are still many things we can't do for our babies while they are here in the NICU, at least not in the traditional sense. This causes some sense of loss and mourning, but as we adjust. We don't really have a choice anyway.

One of the directly impactful things we can do is feed the babies. Correction, it's one of the things *Kylene* can do. I'm still pretty useless in this department. However, since the babies are much too small for traditional nursing, Kylene has to use a breast pump to extract the milk. If you've never witnessed a breast pump in action, it's pretty incredible. Technology intervenes to take a biological miracle of motherhood and makes the mom's body become somewhat utilitarian; a source of nutrition, sort of a spring to be tapped.

From my outside perspective the pumping process can be painful, and repeatedly subjects the mother to an unflattering and vulnerable situation. Yet, working or otherwise busy moms subject themselves to the rigors of this routine all the time for the sake of their babies. They sacrifice their own convenience and comfort in order to provide their babies with the most naturally nutritious sustenance available. This is selflessness defined. These women are amazing. Kylene is superwoman.

Kylene learned the equipment and got started as soon as her body was ready. The setup here is pretty nice and the NICU floor has some special lactation rooms where she can privately use the pump. The milk is collected in her own stash of small plastic jars, which we label with the date and then place the jars in our plastic basket labeled "Smith." The basket is stored in a special mini refrigerator in the NICU family lounge reserved for only breast milk. There aren't many places in the world that can boast a refrigerator that is dedicated solely to breast milk, but we have one here, and the thing is chock full.

Just like the Smith repository, each NICU mom has her own basket with a variety of plastic graduated jars featuring the date of production. At feeding time, the nurses or NICU parents retrieve some milk from the proper basket and feed their matching preemie baby. It's a simple system.

The pumping process itself has a steep learning curve and for us, it starts with a few iterations of understandable frustration and guilt, but now that Kylene has the hang of it, she is able to get a few ounces at a time. It's not perfectly consistent, but it's working. One time it is an ounce, and then maybe two the next try. Regardless, every ounce is a victory and provides nourishment for our babies. As her body adjusts and she becomes more proficient, she slowly works her way up to several ounces per session. She is doing amazing. I help a little at the end and deliver the milk to the fridge. It's basically all I can do, but it's something and though small, it's one less thing for Kylene to have to do.

Off on one of my critically helpful milk delivery errands, as I am stowing the milk in our basket, I can't help but look around at other baskets. Our production is on the lighter end of the spectrum, but it doesn't matter, we could only collect what her body produces and that is that. Though maybe lighter, we are still on the same order of magnitude as the others; like ours, each basket hosts a few partially filled bottles.

This is the case across the fridge, except for one basket. One basket is completely full of full bottles, and there is an additional large container as well, also full. No one else has one of these big jars and this basket must have ten times the amount of milk that we have.

What in the world is going on here? Who is this woman? How tall is she? She must be superhuman, some sort of milk maven.

This production level could lead to a private bottling and distribution center. There is now a way to feed entire villages of malnourished orphan infants. I'm not jealous, I'm just astonished, and kind of impressed. I honestly have no idea who this person is, since we have had extreme tunnel vision these last several days and haven't really met any of the other parents. All I know is the milk maven's basket is full of more milk than the rest of all the other baskets combined. It makes me chuckle and shake my head a little, and I wonder who it is. But for now, the milk maven mystery offers only one clue. The basket is labeled with a single, cryptic word: *Tait*.

Part IX - Leaving

Moving Day

(Day 10 in the NICU)

Arriving at the hospital today, we make our way through our typical entrance routine. Park the car, cross the street on the elevated walkway, down the stairs, enter the building in the northeast corner by the heart center, curve down the hallway past the breakfast place that always seems closed, walk diagonally through the lobby, past the front desk, past the indoor fountain, to the first-floor connecting hallway that yields passage to the old wing of the hospital. Then it's up the elevator to the NICU floor.

We are savvy veterans at this point. We know our way around, we know how things work, and when we see other parents arriving in a cloud of despair and unknown, much like we were a week ago, we can only smile knowingly while our hearts hurt for them.

Finally at our floor, we mindlessly cross the elevator lobby, move straight into the scrub-in station, set down our bags, and take off our watches. We roll up our sleeves, wet and lather our arms, and scrub everything from the elbows to fingertips. Once we finish, we collect our belongings and proceed down the same series of hallways, left at the T, down another hallway and turn again into the NICU. It is all very routine, like clockwork, every move unsurprising and altogether expected. Today is just another day, and everything looks the same except as we enter the room there is one big difference. Our kids aren't here. They aren't just moved over one station like when they moved Roman to be next to Eden. They are *gone*. Minor detail.

A flash flood of concern pours into my mind, and I have a brief instant of internal panic and confusion. I notice a familiar nurse and ask,

"Where are Roman and Eden?"

She had already spotted us and likely read the unveiled expression on my face, or maybe just read my mind because before the words are all the way out of my mouth, she quickly explains,

"They moved them to NIM."

Normally, I'd be displeased. If you've read the book this far, you already know that. I require information and answers at every juncture, and when I don't get that, my reactions are, well, less than subtle.

Why are they changing things without us being consulted? Why didn't someone at least tell us what was happening?

I still want to know those answers, but technically, I asked a question and I have received a very clear answer. They moved them. They aren't here, they are now over there. Over where? The NIM.

The neonatal *intermediate* care unit. Moving there means good things are happening. The panel of neonatology specialists have met, discussed, and due to our twins' progress and development, have granted them a health status upgrade; it is time for Eden and Roman to move on. We have been waiting and hoping for this change, so despite the brief heart palpitations incurred over my missing children, I'm actually happier about the progress milestone than upset about imperfect communication. We are moving up.

And so, just like that, our time in the NICU is over. There is no fanfare, no farewell, and no further discussion needed. We walk out of our NICU room and head back the way we came, with only one thought: *Where exactly is the NIM?*

Of course, I have heard of the NIM before and knew that it was likely the next stop on our journey home, but I have never actually seen it or really thought much about it. Now, suddenly, the NIM has become very real, and we are headed there now, walking with purpose, intent on finding our children.

Kylene seems to have a decent idea of where the NIM is located, so we backtrack to the T in the hallway where we, until now have always turned left toward the NICU. Now, uncharted waters are ahead and this time we turn right to head to NIM. We speed walk down the hall to a large open doorway.

This is it. We enter without hesitation for, regardless of decorum or authorization, we are still on a mission to find our children. As I survey the room, Kylene's motherly senses are activated and in just a few seconds, her homing device locates the kids.

"They are right there," she confirms. Indeed, they are. Exhale. Inhale. Hoo hoo hee. Roman and Eden are here, and they are fine. They are the same, and they don't know anything has changed. But as I look around, I start to notice how the NIM is different from the NICU.

Most staff call this place the "Pavilion." It seems an apt description as the NIM Pavilion is a rather large space, much bigger than the NICU room we just left. I would guess it is twice the size, with double the number of kids. We learn the patient to nurse ratio has jumped from two to one in the NICU to four to one here in the NIM. That detail gives me a little pause, but it does make sense. There are fewer kids here with complex long-term obstacles to overcome. This is a gathering place for the growers and feeders.

The ambience in the Pavilion is different as well. It's livelier here, more rambunctious. There are more human noises—voices and baby sounds—and a little less interruption from beeping alarms. The monitors are still here, but they are more stable and less alarming, both literally and figuratively. Beyond all the nuanced physical changes, the most striking difference is a new sensation. There's a feeling in the air, something perceptible but immeasurable, an undercurrent I didn't feel in the NICU: hope.

The parents here have already been through the worst of it and have come out the other end. Their kids are improving, even if slowly; they're making progress and are on the upward path to success. There are still setbacks, frustration, and days and nights of worrying, but the next step after the NIM is discharge. The next step is home, and it is tantalizingly within reach.

Underestimated

(Day 11 in the NICU)

With the correct birth date sorted out and the unexpected transition to NIM complete, both babies are supposedly done with gavage and are authorized to bottle feed. That sounds like a victory, and it is, but bottle feeding is harder than it sounds. Their little brains are still just on the edge of being able to regulate the suck, swallow, and breathe sequence. It's not a foregone conclusion that they will succeed on any given day or at any given feeding. There are benchmarks, both for total volume consumed and total time to consume it. It's a race against the clock. If you make it, congratulations kid, you've drunk enough to meet the daily nourishment quota. Nothing happens other than you've made your parents happy and secured yourself a full belly. If you can't take it all, or you can't do it fast enough, you get the auxiliary reward—a gavage tube to finish your feeding. If that happens, it feels like a demotion or a punishment. It's not really, it's just a way to get them the food they need, but it feels like a shortcoming anyway.

Eden is good at feeding. She doesn't like to waste a lot of time, so she gets right to business and sucks it all down, meets her quota, and heads back to her busy schedule of sleeping. It's almost as if she knows the requirements and always makes the milk volume and the time duration with plenty of room to spare.

Roman is a different story. First, he is smaller, so he can't handle quite as much volume. More critical, he isn't as focused on the task at hand and has no sense of urgency. That is the most understated way to put it. Whatever the absolute opposite of urgency is, that's his demeanor. There is always something else to see or do, a joke to laugh at or gas to pass, and the required consumption volumes and times seem more like loose suggestions to him, when he's interested at all. I swear sometimes he just forgets entirely that he is drinking from a bottle and then is surprised to find it in his mouth. He's going to do it on his own terms, or maybe not at all, and he'll get there if and when it suits him. This situation leaves us frustrated, because we believe he can do it, but either he doesn't have the stamina to finish, or he just doesn't care. The posture has earned him the auxiliary reward a few times. The twenty-minute hourglass elapses and he hasn't completed a whole ounce, so we have to resort to the gavage option. He still gets the nourishment he needs, and he's still growing, but it always feels like a setback anyway.

We recommit ourselves to helping him try, so the next several feedings we work toward keeping him engaged. With positive encouragement and deliberate focus management, he easily drinks his ounce in record time. We've logged a new data point of proof that he *can* do this. Then the next feeding, he's back to his old ways, and seems intent on doing anything but focusing on drinking. I work with him the entire time frame and with moments to spare, he re-engages and barely finishes the ounce. Whereas Eden seems to know what is needed and completes it promptly to get it over with, Roman also seems to know, but he deliberately strings it out until the dramatic last moment. A fully capable procrastinator. It's almost as if he knows what I want him to do, and he holds out just to amplify my stress levels.

The close finishes continue for the next day, but generally, if either Kylene or I are feeding him, Roman makes the goal pretty regularly. If the nurses feed him, it's a crapshoot as they don't know how to keep him on task. That's probably not true and maybe unfair. They all work here so I'm sure they've probably seen similar situations and they know all the tricks. And to be fair, many of the nurses are his greatest cheerleaders and are immensely helpful to him, Eden, and to us.

However, there are other nurses, and one in particular who is not my favorite. She is less patient and isn't interested in the extra effort it takes to help him toward success. Unfortunately, when she's assigned to our kids, she's also the lord of the stopwatch. She tries the feeding, she records the results, and she decides whether or not he has succeeded at his task. Based on past results, when she is on duty, he never makes it, and gavage always happens. This is not a fruitful partnership.

Just my luck, Not-My-Favorite nurse is on duty again today and she announces it's time for Roman's next feeding. I get everything ready, and get started, and he's doing everything right, but also making no progress whatsoever. He's not zoning out or doing any of his normal avoidance tactics either, the milk level just isn't moving, not even a little. Not-My-Favorite notices the struggle and puts down the charting clipboard.

"See. He just can't do it. You're pushing too hard, and he just can't do it. He's not ready."

As she offers her dismissive words with a heavy hint of contempt, she stands up and walks back to her station, effectively declaring the bottle-feeding session to be over. I'm frustrated by the inexplicable performance but more irritated by her attitude. Even if he is struggling, we could use some support. I might not deserve it, but I'm quite certain Roman does. He doesn't need that kind of negativity.

In a final act of frustration, I revisit all the variables. His head position, body angle, and everything seems right. I tap the rubber nipple of the tiny bottle against my arm and… nothing. The little telltale drip that we're all used to seeing doesn't materialize.

That's weird.

I unscrew the top and look down into the nipple from the inside and discover a large clump of formula.

The nipple is clogged!

I quickly manipulate the end, clear the blockage, and rush over to Not-My-Favorite.

"The bottle was clogged. That's why he wasn't drinking. That's not his fault. Let him try again," I contend.

She forcefully responds. "He just can't do it. He can try again tomorrow or maybe the next day."

I'm not giving up on him and I'm certainly not giving away two more days. No way.

"Yes, he can, he's been doing it the last several days. The bottle was clogged, that's all. Restart the clock."

My last phrase is not a negotiation, it is a statement, if not a demand. We are restarting the clock. I sit back down with the now cleared bottle, scoop up Roman, and we try again. He chugs it down like a champ, consuming more milk than required and in record time. He can do it. He *did* do it, again, despite Not-My-Favorite's misgivings.

After he finishes, I set him back down, smugly walk over to Not-My-Favorite with the empty bottle and announce the exemplary time Roman just made.

Write it down.

She does so, begrudgingly but then mentions to me yet again that she doesn't think he can do it.

Frankly, I don't care what you think.

I leave the NIM, walk down the hall, and for the second time, I ask to speak to the charge nurse. When she arrives, she is helpful and responsive to my request: I don't want Not-My-Favorite nurse to be assigned to either of my kids. There are plenty of excellent, caring nurses here—I don't need one who doesn't believe in my kid or isn't willing to work with him to succeed. I don't want her around anymore. And so, it is done.

I'm really not making many friends.

Connections

(Day 12 in the NICU)

After a few days in the NIM, we start noticing some of the same people coming and going in rhythms similar to our own. Every night around 6:30 pm, Kylene and I take a break from our kid interactions and go to the family lounge to rest and eat dinner together. Occasionally, we grab something from the cafeteria, but usually it's something we've packed from home. It's a nice room with a kitchen to heat up food, room to sit at an actual table, and space to relax for a few minutes and have a private conversation. Naturally, we mostly talk about the kids, but as they continue to improve and our stress levels decrease, we start to notice other people and talk about them in sort of a "guess their situation" type of game.

Kylene is very good at this game, and it turns out, I am terrible at it. She has somehow noticed and cataloged every mom in a three-county radius, estimated their age, and dreamt up some life scenario for each of them. Then, she can identify the accompanying dad for the mom, and it only help her extend the imaginary story further. As entertaining as our little fictional gossip game has become, the scary part is that her powers of observation are so keen that her imagined synopsis for each couple seems quite plausible, if not precisely accurate. I find I'm of no help to either contradict or corroborate the stories, because I haven't noticed most of these people. I don't even know who she's talking about most of the time. I guess I've been so busy thinking about myself and our situation, I haven't paid any attention to most of the people around here.

There is one person I have noticed simply because I've seen her several times. It started when we were in the NICU. Every time I was in the family lounge I would see this same woman. She seemed to be a NICU mom, about our age, and she would always walk through the lounge and put her milk in the special fridge. She had long brown hair, and she always smiled. I noticed that mainly because I wasn't smiling much that first week, but she always did. It was a kind gesture, and it was memorable.

The only other person I noticed was this tall, thin guy who occasionally sauntered through the lounge, and oddly he would always smile too. I didn't know what he was so happy about, but he smiled, and I remembered that. I never saw either of them anywhere but in the lounge. Granted, it's not like I was popping my head in all the other rooms looking for strangers, but I just never saw either of them anywhere else.

Now we have moved into the NIM, and lo and behold, there is the smiling gal on the other side of the room, and wouldn't you know it, the smiling guy is with her.

Ohhhh. They go together. They are a smiling couple.

Now that those dots are connected, we can begin to imagine what their life story is and discuss it fictitiously over our lounge dinners.

Kylene and I head to the lounge tonight and find that Team Smile is already in there eating their own meal. We exchange smiles (our offerings are, of course, inadequate compared to Team Smile) and then begin to exchange verbal pleasantries as well.

We learn the smiling woman's name is Kendra, her smiling husband's name is Jamie, and they are completely and utterly… normal. As the conversation continues, we discover they are nearly the same ages as us, they too live in Rockford, they met in high school, he's an engineer, she's a math teacher, and they have boy-girl fraternal twins who were born at 30 weeks and 6 days. This is all too eerily familiar. We've just met ourselves, albeit with better smiles, and they are exactly one week ahead of us on this journey.

We continue to see them throughout the day and into the next day, now able to greet each other by name instead of just a smile. Before we know it, we've actually made some friends. This is the last thing I was expecting to happen, but connecting with such nice people feels really good. As Kylene and Kendra begin making plans and exchange phone numbers I ask,

"I know it's Kendra and Jamie, but what's your last name?"

"It's Tait. Kendra and Jamie Tait."

Oh my goodness. It's her. It's the Milk Maven!

I exchange a quick knowing glance with Kylene and then before she can forbid it with her eyes, I unceremoniously blurt out,

"Wait, Tait? You're the one with the basket full of milk?"

Kendra sheepishly shrugs and smiles, "Yes."

Kylene jovially queries, "How are you doing that? I can't get more than a few ounces!"

"I don't know what's happening, it just keeps coming!"

"We've got gallons of it," Jamie confirms.

We are all laughing, nearly hysterically, at the absurdity of the unknowns of milk production volumes. I hope I haven't embarrassed our new friend, but I don't think I have. We are just bonding over the fact that none of us really has a clue about we are doing, but this is our current situation. Sharing that confusion with someone else who knows just how it feels is liberating, joyous, welcomed, and needed so much more than I realized. Kylene can commiserate with Kendra, and I can do the same with Jamie. We can check in and compare. We can advocate and cheer for their twins and they for ours. It is a blessing, a bond emerging from a time of strife and uncertainty. No matter what happens, they will forever be the cherished friends we met in the NICU. The ones who smiled first. The mavens with all the milk.

Three More

(Day 18 in the NICU)

It has been over two weeks since the kids were born and a week since we shifted over to the NIM. Our experience here is going well, and the daily routine has become, well, rather routine.

Eden and Roman are stable, progressing rapidly, and are generally hitting all the marks for feeding volumes, weight gain, heat regulation, and every other development milestone. Gone are my days of endless worry and stress about monitors and alarms. Replacing those concerns are new frustrations about the next steps of the plan, general communication from the medical team, and details about how many more days or weeks they'll have to stay.

It's a strange transformation, this metamorphosis we've undertaken. Two weeks ago I was clinging to every medical team member and every device, imploring them to help my kids and make everything okay. Now, I am ready to cast off the shackles of hospital procedures and bring these babies home. Kylene has the routine completely under control and I think even I can handle it. Are we still overwhelmed at times? Yes. Exhausted constantly? Likely. Even so, I'm comfortable and confident we will be fine and frankly, I'm anxious to leave. We are now purely in the waiting game. Waiting for the medical staff to grant our graduation out of the NICU.

Both babies are over four pounds, veritable behemoths now compared to their starting weight, but they are still tiny by normal birth weight standards. We hear rumors that no one leaves the NICU unless they're over five pounds. If that is true, our departure is still a long way away. However, the rounding neonatologists have been hinting otherwise. Even Dr. Doctor (gimme the news) himself suggested we could potentially leave in three or so days. Regardless of how definitive he meant to be with that statement, his words offer a glimmer of hope I'm interpreting as a shining beacon. It allows me to draw a line in the sand and establishes a tangible goal to achieve. I begin to schedule a homecoming, or rather, a homegoing.

This is something near, something attainable, something for me to look forward to. We had visions of Christmas in the NICU and then in the NIM, because we thought we would be here until February. This new timeline could put us home before Christmas, which would be so incredible it's hard to let myself imagine it. No more nebulous thresholds - they need to be over five pounds, they must reach their full gestational age, or whenever Not-My-Favorite thinks it is possible. No more of that. A specific answer was given. Three more days.

Adamant Anne

(Day 19 in the NICU)

I take the departure projections seriously, and each day I consult the rounding doctor confirming the statuses haven't changed. The doctors' responses typically land somewhere between a strong affirmation of the timeline and subtle reservation that they might agree. These are not super reassuring, but there has been no indication of a "no" either, and no retractions or corrections of a misperception. I take all these as good signs.

We are in the final stretch, we'll be leaving soon, and as exciting as that is, I'm beginning to process what that really means. All this nursing care will cease, and there will be no one to ask, no one to defer to, and no one to rely on when we have questions or need help. That is a little scary, but we have had a lot of time here to learn and we've asked a lot of questions. I think I've asked every possible question.

The shift won't be all that abrupt since Kylene really does most of the work now anyway. The main difference is, right now, if we want to slip out and eat dinner, we can just leave. If Kylene needs to pump or do anything, and I'm at work, she just goes and does it. Once we are home, that charade of convenience will end. There will be two babies' needs to tend to and very little room for anything like going to the bathroom, or resting, eating or showering. Such things must be squeezed into the fleeting moments of two precarious and misaligned nap cycles or, more likely, they will just have to wait until reinforcements arrive.

I am the reinforcements. I will take some time off to be home so we can tag team the twins with a man-to-man defense. I won't be home forever, which means she will have to be able to handle them alone, but I'm certain she'll be fine. Kylene herself will also have to leave the house eventually, meaning I'll be left alone with the double team action from time to time. It won't be mom-level care, but I'm up to the challenge.

Certainly, it will all be difficult, but it will be at home. No nurses or doctors, and our world will be free of hospital equipment, monitor screens, other patients, intercom announcements, and other distractions. We will get to take care of our kids, in our house, with our things and comforts, in the place where our family belongs. All of us.

As we prepare for the pending reality of leaving, we begin to assemble our things and are graciously given a lot of diapers and formula and other gear that will help us get started. We also will take home a valuable but intangible gift — the built-in schedule the hospital follows that our babies are already accustomed to. We plan to maintain it as closely as possible because, well, I like plans and this one has been proved to work. Without a plan, this could quickly unravel into chaos, so the schedule stays. The last thing we are receiving in what we hope are our final days here is unexpected advice from Anne.

Anne is a lifelong friend of our friend Kim, the one we met for dinner the day we found out about the twins. Anne is a NICU nurse here at our hospital, and when the babies were born, Kim hooked us up with Anne. She was a blessing from day one. Even though Anne is only a friend of a friend, she is a friendly face and a stabilizing force bringing knowledge and a personal touch to our situation. In some of our roughest patches, she has given us an inside partner, advocating for us and our kids, and she has periodically swooped in with clarity and insight. I always feel best if Anne is rotated onto our kids, and she has several times. Those were the nights I slept best, knowing Anne was taking care of them.

Anne always speaks with self-assured confidence and is not shy with her opinions, but we welcome her opinions. We often need them in our moments of uncertainty, and many times her strong voice of direction proved quite helpful.

Now that we are poised to leave, Anne has serious parting words for us. She begins with a detailed description and warning about the next foe that lurks in the shadows: Respiratory Syncytial Virus, or RSV. Though a seemingly passive virus which brings mild cold-like symptoms to the healthy, it can deliver serious, even life-threatening complications to the frail, such as the elderly or infants. That's us. This is the monster against whom we need to protect Roman and Eden. They are tough and have endured much, but they are still slight, tiny humans for whom infections and viruses can be troubling, even deadly. It's a legitimate concern, but honestly, it's one that wasn't on my radar.

As my anxiety levels rise, Anne draws our attention to another reality of which we hadn't been aware. She informs us that the proverbial NICU doors are one-way; You can leave but you can't come back, ever. Once the kids have been out in the real world, if they get sick or weak or need care for whatever reason, we don't get to come back to the friendly confines of the sterile NICU. It is just too dangerous for the highly susceptible population of infant newborns to be exposed to outside contamination and infection. It makes sense; if our babies contract RSV, they certainly can't come in here and risk spreading it around to everyone else.

Of course, we can come back and get help if needed, but if we do, even if the babies are still only four pounds and we feel like they belong in the NICU, we will have to go to the PICU. The Pediatric Intensive Care Unit. We could still get great care there, but PICU is for everyone from returning infants up through age eighteen. That would be a completely different dynamic, one that we want to avoid. Imagine my RSV-laden infant in a room with or across the hall from a high school senior battling some severe infection. I wish that other imaginary kid well, but no thanks. The NICU would seem downright heavenly compared to that.

Anne's admonishment comes full circle. We don't want RSV because we don't want to come back to the hospital, so if we simplify the equation further, it comes down to one thing. Don't let them get sick. Period. It is December, winter in Michigan, the height of cold and flu season. This is not a small concern and not a small task.

Anne is adamant that we need to be vigilant about hand washing, restricting visitors, and doing everything we can to protect the kids. She thoroughly convinces us and leaves us convicted with a not-so-slight aftertaste of fear. The fear of RSV, the fear of returning to the hospital, and the fear of failing our kids. And I might be just a little afraid of Anne now too, or of what she will do to me if we get RSV. Regardless, the warnings are dire, but instructive, and we plan to heed them.

Split Decision

(Day 21 in the NICU)

The three days of waiting passed, and the final countdown is over. It is departure day. The heat at home is turned up, the car seat bases are installed and ready, and we're all set with a plan for a late afternoon dismissal. We both woke up today feeling anxious but energized and ready for the transition. Today is the start of the next chapter of life.

My office Christmas party lunch potluck is scheduled for today at noon, and since it's generally good practice to show up at things like this, and since I actually like my coworkers, I'm hoping to attend. Our plan is for me to go into the office in the morning, work a few hours, participate in the potluck, and then head to the hospital to pick up my family and go home. It sounds surreal even saying it, but it's happening. I can't believe it. Today is the day.

My morning at work is busy and I try to keep my mind off of what's coming this afternoon, but I'm failing miserably. Going home with the kids is all I can think about. I haven't accomplished much billable work, but it's okay, I'm way ahead of goal for the year anyway, even with all the time away for baby stuff. Aside from my personal distractions, the aromas of various crockpot offerings waft through our dingy, undersized cubicle farm and into my office, luring my mind in ever more unfocused directions.

Finally, mercifully, the potluck begins and I'm in line to fill my blue plastic plate with samplings of meatballs, crackers and cheese, Cincinnati-style chili, copious amounts of chips, and some obligatory raw carrots with an extremely unhealthful spinach dip. I'm hungry and excited to partake of the veritable smorgasbord as well as enjoy a few minutes with my colleagues. I have just found an awkward folding chair at the large rectangular table when suddenly my phone rings.

It's Kylene. I answer anxiously and before she even speaks, I can hear that she is crying. I am instantly on high alert. Her crying is always a concern, but when my infant children live in the hospital and exist only inches away from the nebulous swirl of impending doom, any unexpected distress crying makes my mind race to places I can't fathom.

"Roman is not coming home," she sobs.

"What! Why not?" I am confused and incensed.

"The doctor said he's not ready."

Inhale. Exhale. It seems he's okay, no new major issues have emerged, but this is still a monumental disappointment.

"Okay, so we stay another day, we can have them both stay." That seems ok to me.

"No, I tried, they won't do that. Eden is being released and can't stay, and Roman is not going. He has to stay behind."

"Ok, I'm leaving now. I'll be right there."

I stand up from my nearly untouched plate, gaze longingly at the food that I'm not going to eat, and release a, long, audible, disappointed, sigh. It's not about the food. Ok, it's a little about the food, it looked really good, but it's mainly about this troubling news. This was not the plan. This was not what we were expecting. The joy of our long-awaited departure day has been bombarded by this scathing attack on our fragile hearts. It leaves us in an unfair limbo.

It's hard to feel good about Eden without feeling horrible about Roman and I don't know how to reconcile the divide. I get in the truck and drive over as quickly as I can. I park in my favorite spot, jog across the parking structure, stride through the lobby and take the elevator up. I'm on autopilot, my body knows the way, and right now I'm dwelling on other things.

I arrive in the NIM, find Kylene and try to console her. Actually, she's doing decently well, considering the circumstances, and like me she is just taking time to process the news. I check in with Eden and relay my veiled excitement for her.

"We get to take you home today!"

My heart is happy for her and proud of how far she has come. This is a good day and a wonderful accomplishment.

I check in with Roman and my heart breaks. More sighing. I don't tell him what's happening; not that he would understand anyway, but I greet him and talk to him about other non-critical things. I'm doing my best to not push my negativity and disappointment onto him. He doesn't need or deserve any of that. I am happy to see him though and just wish he was coming with us.

Having made my family rounds, I'm compelled to seek out the charge nurse and rounding doctor yet again.

I approach the desk and I surprise myself at my level of composure as I calmly start a pointed conversation.

"Why is Roman not going home today?"

The charge nurse knows me, she knows what has transpired, and she knows I'm disappointed, but she summons a sensitive, measured response.

"The doctor feels he needs more time. He had one brady today and we'd like to see him a little heavier."

With unexpected restraint that leaves me feeling rather impressed with myself in the moment I reply, "I'm not questioning the doctors' medical decisions. I want what is best for Roman and if they say he needs to stay, then that's what we're doing. I am questioning the inconsistency of information we've been given. We've been told repeatedly, for several days, that they are both going home today and that hasn't wavered. Now, all of a sudden, you tell us two hours before we're going to leave that he's not ready? That is unacceptable. Nothing has changed. I expect better, more consistent information."

I didn't yell or get visibly angry; I just plainly stated my case. I have repeatedly asked and confirmed the timelines every day, multiple times, precisely to avoid this scenario. I ask questions and seek clarifications because I need information, so I can plan and do my best to prepare. Nevertheless, here we are with a broken plan and crushed spirits.

She acknowledges my complaint, though it's really more of a lament, and I suspect my file has grown a few more millimeters. (Warning, engineer dad is unhappy, again. Do not initiate contact.) I'm still not making many friends here and I think I'm just exhausted with all of it. As much as I want to leave with my kids, I'm guessing the staff are ready for me to leave too.

Our disappointment lingers, but I start to come to terms with the reality of what today is actually going to be. I gather Eden's stuff and prepare for her departure. She's less than three weeks old, and only four pounds, but somehow, I have multiple armloads of things to carry home with us.

Eden is disconnected from everything, no cords, no monitors, no anything. That detachment ushers in a strange new dichotomy. It feels liberating for her to be free and unrestrained, but at the same time, I have a gnawing uncertainty remains because now I don't have constant information and feedback on her vital status. I think I have become reliant on, and maybe even comforted, by the numbers. But even if I think I need the numbers, Eden doesn't. She is fine.

She's out of her isolette for the last time and is now strapped and snuggled in her car seat. She looks so small in what feels like an oversized carrier and it's hard to imagine that she might ever fit in it properly. She is ready. Eden is leaving after twenty-one days in the NICU. However, we are not ready to face the dreaded moment that is rapidly approaching.

After wasting as much time as possible loitering, checking, and rechecking all of our stuff, we turn our attention to Roman and play out our typical evening routine as if everything is the same as it has been the last twenty plus days. We touch his hands and head, whisper several recitations of "good night" and "I love you," and I assure him I'll be right back to see him in the morning. He doesn't know that he's staying and his sister is leaving. In fact, he'll never know or at least he won't remember. It's totally fine. Everything is fine. He's going to be fine. That's what I tell Kylene and that's what I keep telling myself.

Only it's not fine. It's not, because I know, because we know. We know that we are leaving him behind. Leaving him alone in this place that we so desperately needed and that we now even more desperately want to leave. He doesn't know. But I know. I know and it is silently breaking my heart to leave him.

This moment that was supposed to be so unequivocally joyous has become fractured. I am truly thrilled to be taking Eden home. This is cause for celebration. At the exact same instant, my baby boy is not coming home today and that is cause for mourning. It's *City Slickers* all over again. Same moment, same day.

We deliver Eden to the car where I double-check and then triple-check that she's properly secured in the car seat. Kylene sits in the back with Eden, and though she has lingering tears from leaving Roman behind, we muster genuine happiness and excitement in the car as I slowly, extra cautiously, drive home with our most precious cargo.

When we get home, a heavy blanket of incompleteness hangs over us with our family separated in a new and painful way, but we try to make the best of it and enjoy a pleasant evening of having our baby daughter home with us. We take pictures and fuss over her for a while until it's time for bed. Eden will sleep in the cradle, the one my dad made for us, right in our bedroom. It's quaint and feels nearly Rockwellian, except that half of the canvas is blank.

We learn many things within the first few hours of attempted sleep on this first night. Eden's supposed silence in the NICU was a misleading charade. The truth is out: She's noisy. I know this because the highest authority in the room (Kylene) has decreed we can't have our white noise fan on for fear of missing hearing something. It works, and we don't miss anything. I hear Eden's every breath, every tiny cough, every rustling of the cradle, and every unexpected noise. If one of Edens's eyelashes brushes past another one, I hear it. I hear everything.

Following every barely perceptible sound, my mind races with dissection and diagnostics, which half the time raises my heartbeat to near panic mode, and the other half forces me out of bed just to make sure she is okay. I'm not alone in this inaugural journey of parenting ineptitude. We are both doing it. Somehow, Kylene hears ten times the number of things that I hear. Ten times everything equals a lot, so on the unlikely occasion where I may actually drift off to sleep, Kylene hears something new and moves suddenly to listen better or to check on Eden and luckily startles me enough to get me back to being awake and listening. So here we are, both lying in bed, awake, and on high alert, hearing every utterance and minute movement, confirming with each other what we just heard, and then discussing what we heard in concerned, hushed whispers.

"What was that?"

"What are we supposed to do now?"

"How can she be so little and be that noisy?"

"What is she doing?"

Ironically, the NICU schedule has shaped and trained her and Eden sleeps pretty well, at least for an infant. She logs two to three hours at a time, but she can still make noises while she sleeps, which now we are lying awake to catalog and process moment by moment.

I, on the other hand, do not sleep. I barely sleep at all, mostly because I'm hearing and worrying about every sound, and when I'm not worrying, I'm annoyed that I'm still awake and being disturbed by the sounds or being woken up to be asked if I heard that. Then as I'm lying here, awake, worried, and annoyed, I resume thinking about Roman. It all makes for a solid first night.

As I wake up the next morning (or just finally get up, since I was already awake), I'm exhausted and irritated and yet somehow still thrilled and relieved that Eden is here. Her being home is a good thing, despite the fact that her brother is missing. Not only is she here, she's staying here—forever if it's up to me, but at least for the foreseeable future. Kylene is up too and is staying home with Eden for her first official day as the all-everything provider—no nurses, no doctors, no helpers, and no dad. I'm leaving shortly to go back to the hospital. Back to my boy, because he needs me. Well, that's probably not true, he is probably fine and doesn't even know I'm gone. He may not need me, but I need him.

The Retrieval

(Day 22 in the NICU)

It's morning, still quite early, but when sleep is so elusive, time becomes somewhat relative. I am up and showered and ready to go. But, once again, I find myself torn; I don't want to leave Kylene and Eden, but I more so don't want Roman to be alone today. So, I leave and head back to the hospital.

I park and walk in and do all the things I always do, but this time it feels different, more expedient. Once I arrive at the NIM, it feels really different. Kylene isn't here, and Eden isn't here, and that makes it weird, but I'm more relieved than ever to be here. I haven't felt great since we left, and Kylene was very distraught, but being here now, I already feel better, just knowing that I'm here and he's not alone.

Our hospital team roster has changed and so has our posture. It's me and Roman, father and son, a formidable duo. Our first time as just the two of us. We are in this together, and we're not patiently waiting anymore. We are pressing and working toward our collective renewed goal: Exit.

As I unload my lunch and my backpack, the nurses confirm Roman had a good night, and within a few minutes I've got him ready to start his first morning feeding. He downs all the required ounces and seems to be wanting more, so I let him keep going and he is absolutely crushing it. It is time to get moving and get out of this place, and somehow, I think he senses it. He does everything right and does so easily. He has been slowly catching up to Eden and now is right on pace with what she is doing. He is a last-minute warrior. I'm convinced he is ready, but then again, I'm slightly biased.

I spend all day by Roman's side, keeping watch, making sure he gets the custom attention that ensures his success, and enjoying the time with just the two of us. I'm also waiting, rather impatiently, for the rounding doctor to show up. It's a different one every day so I never quite know who it will be or when the doc will swing through. It's like waiting for a cable or power company technician to come and turn on your service — they'll be there sometime between 10:00 am and 2:00 pm. Ugh.

I don't dare leave for anything, not to use the bathroom, or to grab a sandwich, not even water, simply because I don't want to miss the window of time when the doctor is here. I can't risk something being observed, or decided and written in Roman's chart, only for me to be told later with inadequate explanation.

I need to be part of the conversation. I want to discuss everything with the doctor and make sure to inform him of the appropriate facts that I already see. I expect to stop short of trying to convince him of anything, but I need to hear the details personally to understand next steps and strategies for Roman to be ready.

I will insist that those steps align with what is actually happening, how Roman is actually progressing, not what a generalized schedule says should be happening. I am poised and ready, my spine compressed like a jungle cat, ready to spring into action and begin my tactical advocacy for my son.

At last, the doctor enters the NIM and begins systematically making the rounds through each patient in the room. It's all I can do to keep from standing up and beckoning him to please come over here. I don't actually do that, but I want to.

Instead, I'm forced to wait a little longer and refine my plan of attack. He takes his time. He doesn't know I've been waiting all day, though I suspect he can feel my eyes boring holes through his back. He finally arrives at our area, and I brace myself for an epic exchange of wits, intelligence, and a detailed outlay of my medical expertise. This is going to be monumental, an encounter of such generational importance that it is destined to be commemorated with statues, murals, and rich, ornamental tapestries. My mind sizzles with anxious anticipation as the doctor picks up the chart and silently reviews its contents.

"How is Roman doing today?"

The doctor's opening salvo is so deviously subtle that my mind goes blank, I forget all the brilliant words I had been composing, and my entire dissertation is lost to the ether. I barely stitch together a few coherent phrases.

"I think he is doing great. He drank a ton this morning, his weight is improving, and he hasn't alarmed at all today."

Not the eloquence I had foreseen, but I manage to relay all the facts, laced with a little enthusiasm and desperate hope.

The doctor looks up from the chart, looks at me, and smiles. I think he sees me for what I am, or what I'm trying to be, or maybe he sees both. He reads through the facade of strength, the tension beneath the false veil of calm, and recognizes the signs of unwavering — if at times unpleasant — advocacy. He sees the truth: a fractured shell of a man, quite a young man, trying his best but feeling like a failure at every turn, exhausted, desperate and on the verge of breaking. I imagine he sees dads like me every day, but it is no less real today than any other.

"That's good. I think he's doing very well. I think he is ready to go home. Today."

Today. Not since I opened the black and white card in the front yard have I received such good news. Victory surges within me while relief streams into my body. A refreshing drink at an oasis in the midst of desert desperation.

We made it. You did it, buddy. I knew you could do it.

The doctor continues,

"I am still mildly concerned about his bradys, so I'm going to send him home with a monitor. The discharge nurses can show you how to work it."

Slightly disappointing and concerning, but I have known this might be the case for a while, and if he needs it, then so be it, I'll deal with it. At this point, I would take a wheelbarrow full of equipment if I needed to. I just want to get him home.

I call Kylene to share the excitement and we formulate a plan. She wants to come to the hospital and take him home with me, which I understand, but that means either Eden has to come with her or someone has to come watch Eden. Since we don't want Eden leaving the house for any reason, we need help. It's her first day home from the hospital and we already need a babysitter.

Kylene calls my parents. Can you come to our house and watch your granddaughter? Oh, and you'll get to hold her for the first time. And then see and hold Roman when he gets home.

Unsurprisingly, they agree and leave for our house right away. My parents always come through. They're my parents.

Less than two hours later, Kylene and I are both at the hospital gathering all of Roman's gear, just like yesterday. This iteration of packing is decidedly more joyful because no one is staying behind, and we'll soon all be together.

As we make the final preparations, the staff notify us that Roman is too small for his car seat. So was Eden, in my opinion, but her weight notched her just above some unknown threshold such that she was allowed to use the seat. Roman will instead need a special car bed. I wonder where I am supposed to get that, but before I verbalize the question, the staff show up with one in their hands. It's just like a car seat, but he's laying down, there is a five-point harness and the whole thing is padded. It seems pretty similar to what the car seat would do, but whatever, I don't care, we'll do whatever we need to do. Let's go home.

We exit the NIM pavilion, traverse down the hall, head back to the elevator, and we leave the NICU for the final time. It's December 22nd, Roman has been here for twenty-two days, Eden was here for twenty-one. We are going home. All of us. Home for Christmas.

Thank you, God.

Petting Zoo

Roman coming home is pivotal for our well-being as parents. We did the separated thing for less than twenty-four hours and it was absolutely brutal. It just felt wrong. Not only were the kids separated from each other which we didn't like, but Kylene and I were separated and each trying to make do on our own. We quickly learned; we are better together.

Once we brought him home, Roman received the royal treatment for the day, just like his sister had, but his homecoming was much more joyous, again because we had much to celebrate. As promised, Grandpa and Grandma got to see him and hold him for the first time too. It was a wonderful, heartwarming event, even though it came three weeks late, or six weeks early, depending on how you look at it. Either way, it was perfect, and we needed it.

Now we begin night two of parenting at home and bedtime is once again upon us. Eden proved last night she's too noisy to be in our room but aside from keeping us awake, she did just fine. We move her to the nursery, but Roman takes his turn sleeping in the cradle in our room, just to make things fair and because, naturally, we're a little more worried about him since he's smaller and has the monitor.

Here we go again, fingers crossed for more quiet and more sleep. But, thirty minutes in, things are already vastly different. The era of Roman occupation has begun. Eden's surprising night noises yesterday were funny, and maybe a little annoying, but were like a gentle whisper compared to the cacophony of sounds Roman is emitting. Somehow, he has a way of channeling goat or alpaca sounds. Over, over, and over.

When those noises momentarily subside, it only makes way for some other sound. He does nothing without some sort of audible accompaniment to his thoughts or movements. Whether sleeping or awake, moving or still, there is an ever-present, continuous stream of blabbering.

It's almost comical how absurd this is. You would guess there are multiple animals in the room with us right now, looking for friends or calling out to their mothers, but no, it's just him. Just one four-pound baby boy exhibiting his normal temperament. Oh, and there is one other bonus feature to his night routine, it seems that in our fifteen-minute journey from the hospital to home, Roman inverted his previously established circadian rhythms so that he is now nocturnal. It's time for bed? Nope. He's awake and alert and ready to practice his animal impersonations. It's going to be a long night.

It was a long night. People have these cozy stories about how the sweet baby slept in their room for a year, or how the baby sleeps in their bed. No way. There is none of that for us. We lasted precisely one night with him and then it was off to the nursery to bother his twin sister. To this day, I don't know why we put them in the same room. Maybe it was the novelty of two cribs and them being roommates, or maybe we were clinging to some pointless notion of having a guest room available in our house. For whatever reason, we put them together. While it made for lots of twins memories, it sure didn't make sense from a disruption standpoint. Poor Eden had just one night of peace. After that, the alpaca moved in, and life was never the same.

The Monitor

According to the NICU heart monitor equipment, Roman's bradys —you know, when his heart just stops sometimes—were still occurring periodically. As a result, the conditional NICU release required Roman to come home with a tether. Two chest pads with electrode leads that gather into a plastic cord which is plugged into an AC-powered heart monitor with battery backup. The nurse had shown me how to place the leads and run the machine. It is a little frustrating that he needs it, and when we move him around, we have to bring his bag along, but it's not that hard, and it's worth it if the monitor keeps him safe.

Ironically, the monitor doesn't have a monitor screen, so there's no dashboard for me to watch and pour over every detail. There are just a few LED-type lights on a thin interface which conveys very little actual information. The monitor is really just a remote data logger. It tracks his heart activity and notes if a brady has occurred. Then every week, some retired gentleman drives to our house, plugs in a data transfer tool, and reads the collected information from the logger. It serves as a weekly report card, and we are told how many bradys Roman had that week and how long he has to keep the monitor. The goal is to have a week, or several, with no brady readings, and then we can retire the monitor.

The monitor also serves as an alarm. If there is a brady, it beeps. Not an alarm clock or kitchen timer type of beep, more like a smoke alarm chirp. The intent of the alarm is to tell me his heart has stopped, and I need to go wake it up, so the alarm has to be loud. But it's not only loud, it is soul-piercing. The first brady happened on the second or third night, in the middle of the night. The alarm sounded and woke me from a dead sleep. I could have been asleep in the next county over and I would have heard it. The sound of that alarm is disturbing for all the normal reasons: its pitch, volume, and its general unexpectedness—but more so due to the dire implications. When it sounds, I hear:

Your son might be dying unless you do something. Right. Now.

I was moderately fast in sports. I made the JV soccer team in high school because in tryouts we had a tournament bracket of sprints. I didn't win the whole thing, but I made it to the final group of six or so. My point is, I was decently fast before, but when that alarm sounds and my head is screaming, I am out of bed, sprinting barefoot across the carpet, in nothing but my underwear, moving at world-record speed. Upon my arrival, I tap Roman's shoulder, rub his back, and do whatever I can think of to jump start his heart. Then once it's done, I drag myself back to bed, lie down, and as my pulse decrescendos, the worry resumes, and I lie awake saturated in a pool of fear-driven adrenaline. This is not a healthy existence for me. This is miserable.

The next night, it's going off again and this time, no matter what I do, I can't get it to stop. I strip off his double layers of pajamas with the intent of directly rubbing his skin, only to discover the lead has become disconnected. Lovely. It seems like there should be a different tone to indicate the wire is loose. It might be nice to distinguish a message of "small adjustment needed" from the one signaling "death is only moments away."

The bradys don't happen often, but they do happen, so when the data guy comes, I know the report won't be clean. He tells me how many there were, which is always way more than expected (I'm charting each incident in a spreadsheet. Don't act like you're surprised). The discrepancy is intriguing because if I write down every alarm, even when it's just the leads accidentally coming off, and there are more data points of bradys than what I've recorded, that means the alarm is not sounding for every brady.

How can that be? Or I'm not hearing it, which is impossible. What's the point of the machine if it doesn't sound the alarm every time?

My data guy doesn't have answers, he just downloads the information and then a specialist confirms that Roman needs the monitor for another week.

Over the next few weeks, the alarm keeps going off here and there, and each time it happens, I get a little more removed from worry of his impending heart attack-related death and slide further into being irritated that another alarm means another week of the monitor. I've come to several conclusions. First, I'm not convinced the monitor picks up everything—I have hard evidence of that. Second, I think he self-regulates, and my actions do very little to correct the brady. Third, and this is by far the most important conclusion: I hate that monitor.

Tonight, I'm turning the page and going to sleep with a renewed sense of optimism. I'm predicting no alarms, and it's going to be a good night. But around 2:00 a.m., I'm startled awake by the claxon call. I race to the nursery, tap his shoulder, and rub his back, but nothing works. I'm also trying to be cognizant of my other sleeping infant in the same room so while I want Roman to be okay, I also want this stupid monitor to shut up. It won't stop. I scoop up Roman and the monitor and leave the room to diminish the disturbance for Eden and Kylene. I run down the stairs to the main floor and continue to the other end of the house in the laundry room - the room where I almost passed out the night of my kidney stone escapade. We have a changing table set up in here. I lay Roman on the pad, with the monitor still screeching, strip off his double pajamas, and find the leads are securely in place. I adjust and reattach them anyway, just in case. Still screeching and it's getting to me. I turn the machine off and unplug the leads. Still screeching. I toggle the machine back on and reset it. Still screeching.

My temperature is rising.

Is something wrong with Roman? He seems fine.

I check his pulse in multiple places. Strong. I feel his heartbeat on his chest. Strong and regular. Roman is crying, the monitor is still screeching and I'm scrambling. I tear the panel off the back and find the battery and remove it. The monitor continues screeching.

Kylene arrives from upstairs to investigate the commotion.

"What are you doing? Is he ok?"

"I don't know! I think he's fine, but I can't get this thing to turn off! I don't know what else to do. Check him and see what you think."

She does a similar routine to what I've already done and comes to the same conclusion.

"I think he's ok."

"Me too, I'm taking this thing off."

I take the machine, and the removed battery, and I put it in the garage until it stops beeping. There must be some double safety feature within the machine that has a charged capacitor which will power the unit even without a plug or a battery. I get it. I get why the monitor would have that, but I need that machine to turn off. It's a miracle I didn't smash it to a million pieces. I almost certainly did the wrong thing, but I need a break. I hate that monitor.

When our retired data guy comes later in the week, I show him the log of entries and then he downloads the readings. He asked me what happened on this one day for this period of time. I tell him, in a very matter of fact manner, that is when I disconnected the monitor.

"For how long?"

"I don't know, for several hours. Until it stopped beeping."

That was the last week of the monitor. He hasn't had a brady since.

Notice

As soon as we got both babies home, I got right to business on updating our family blog with some new rules and I printed off a sign which I posted on the front door:

Notice: Susceptible Preemie Infants Inside. To curb any potential problems, the number of visitors will be limited, handwashing will be mandatory and holding babies will be open to grandparents only. If you or anyone in your household is sick or have been in the last 48 hours, we kindly ask that you postpone your visit until you and those you're in contact with are healthy. Thank you for your understanding. Any questions or problems, take it up with the management, a.k.a. Dad.

My sister is none too happy with this declaration as she openly laments to me that her household probably likely won't be illness-free for six months. Her kids are seven and three and some of my favorite people in the world, but they are kids. They have germs, they go to school, and they always have colds. I can't risk it. I *won't* risk it. If they're sick, they can't come, and neither can she.

A group of people from church graciously start a meal train for us. This happens for most young families when they have a baby. It is a lovely gesture and greatly appreciated and the train usually lasts a week or two. With twins, I think everyone feels sorry for us, so the meal train goes on way longer than normal. Many times, people we've never met arrive unexpectedly with a nice meal for us. Upon delivery, the kind and generous soul nearly always has eyes of anticipation, expecting an obligatory baby viewing and maybe even a baby holding session. I get it, people love babies. But I just stand at the door and make no move or invitation to see the babies. Some people even ask if they can come in. I have to always turn them down as politely as I can.

No, sorry, you can't bring your germs in here, but thanks for the lasagna. I'll put it in the freezer with the other eleven we already have.

I don't love the posture I'm taking, and I am thankful for the food (though I despise lasagna), but I'm determined to keep the germs to a minimum and protect my kids.

We stay put for Christmas, we skip all the family gatherings (there are ten this year), and we just stay home. Just the four of us. No hecticness, no racing around with obligations, nothing. It is the most glorious and meaningful Christmas that I can remember, because I have my family at home and we're together. My parents come a few times, including Christmas Day, and other family members visit periodically, but we keep the rules in place. If you're sick, don't come, and unless you're a grandparent, you're not holding babies, at least not for a little while.

***

The twins make it to springtime without getting sick and they get chunkier along the way. We avoided the risk, dodged the RSV, and only went to regular scheduled checkups, with no returns to the hospital. Sorry to everyone we deferred or disregarded. Sorry to my sister and sorry to all those nice ladies who brought us lasagna. I hope you'll forgive me. We made it, and they didn't get sick. The plan worked.

Thanks Anne.

PSAs

This brief interlude from the saga comes as a public service announcement and a general awareness campaign. You're welcome.

Caution, much of what I'm about to share may remind you of something you have done or said yourself. It's over, you did it, and there's no point in worrying about it now. My challenge to you is this: Be better and smarter going forward. We all have our moments of idiocy, but let's do our best to limit them.

With that, my soapbox is firmly situated so I'm going to climb up there for a minute. Bear with me.

Pregnant Pause

Most of us know by now, likely from an awkward experience we stumbled into, that we shouldn't be asking someone about their pregnancy unless we are one hundred percent certain that they are indeed pregnant. Oh, but you think you know for sure? You still shouldn't ask. It's going to end badly eventually.

My personal policy on this topic is absolute. Unless you tell me you're pregnant—and let's face it, you're going to tell me because you're excited about it, and rightly so, and that's what expectant parents do—I'm not going to ask about it. I don't assume anything. In fact, I intentionally assume the opposite. In my mind you're not pregnant. Aside from you being in active labor and you're shouting for someone to come help you because you're having a baby, I'm just thinking you had a big lunch.

If you're not sure, don't ask. There's nothing but trouble for you behind that door.

General Patton

Regardless of whether you don't know for sure if that person is pregnant (see previous rant) or if they have deliberately told you so, you don't have a license to do or say anything else besides offer verbal congratulations. Specifically, you have no social access pass to touch another person's body without explicit invitation. You say you would never do that; nobody would do that. I'm glad you think so, because it means you maintain a shred of faith in humanity, but I'm here to tell you, you're wrong.

I'm convinced that pregnancy of other people, even strangers, elicits some unknown airborne pheromone that compels some people to randomly touch a pregnant belly, uninvited.

Excuse me to the senior boss guy who is fifteen years older than my wife or the random old guy in the grocery store: is there a reason you're touching my wife's very obviously pregnant belly? Was this a habit you exhibited before she was pregnant? Either way, I've got issues with what you're doing, and I'm pretty sure she does too, so stop. This is not normal behavior and it's not okay. Don't do it.

Yes, there is a baby (or two) in there and we all love babies, but there is still something around the baby, namely my wife's uterus and her belly and skin and her clothes. There are several barrier layers, none of which are areas to which you've been, or will ever be, granted access. Oh, but she's your close friend? Nope. No, no, it's fine because you are both women? Still weird. A rapidly expanding waistline is odd enough for my wife, she doesn't need some sort of boundary defying incursion from every good-natured person she meets along the way. If you shouldn't be touching strangers' or friends' bodies when they're not pregnant (and no, you shouldn't), then there is no reason for that to change when a bun is in the oven. Don't touch the oven.

Statistically Questionable

Let me start this subsection by boring you with some statistics. Last time I checked, without medical intervention, around 1 in 250 pregnancies results in twins. It's not crazy uncommon, nothing like lottery-winning odds, but it's still somewhat rare.

Numbers notwithstanding, once you become a parent of multiples, or if you are a multiple yourself, you become more aware of other multiples. It seems like they're all over the place, and suddenly it doesn't seem that unique. In my small office of twenty-five or so people at my first job in Chicago, several of us were all around the same age, sort of growing up together. Over the course of ten years, four of us from that office had twins. Three of us are men and one a woman, but I connect it directly to the fact that we ate at Chipotle together a lot. The barbacoa is what got us. That seems as stupid or as plausible as any other explanation. Tell me I'm wrong. (I am). I digress.

Anyway, once you join the expecting multiples club, another all-too-common situation arises. Questions emerge. I call them the "entitlement of knowledge" questions. They come and continue more prevalently than you can imagine and from absolutely everyone.

Question 1: "Oh you're having twins?" or "You have twins?"

It's a simple answer. "Yes, we are having twins" or "Yes, we do have twins." As a wily veteran of this conversation, let me strongly advise that this is usually an excellent place for you the questioner to end your line of inquiry, because the next few questions, and they're always the same, unravel on a steep and very slippery slope. Further, what comes next is also quite revealing, about you. Trust me, you don't want that either. Let's break down the avoidable questions a little further.

Question 2: "Do twins run in your family?"

If you're asking the dad this question, then sorry Sherlock, you're already off the scent. Basic biology taught us all in the fourth grade, and again in the tenth grade, that humans have eggs and sperm. You don't get two babies without two eggs (fraternal twins) or one egg splitting (identical twins). It's all in the eggs. The dad has nothing to do with either of those scenarios. (Unless unprotected childhood crotch x-rays gave you super, egg-splitting powers, but that's incredibly rare.) So, here's my answer when you ask this one:

"Yes, twins do run in my family; I have an aunt and uncle who are also fraternal twins, but that has nothing to do with my twins."

My tone will most likely imply that I think you should already know that last part. Don't ask this question to dad. Don't make me be mean to you.

Question 3: "Are they identical?"

This is the question I've heard the most. If my children are right in front of you, clearly one being a boy and one being a girl, then you've already lost the game show tonight. There's the door, and please enjoy your parting gifts. If you're just learning I have twins and know no other details and my kids aren't right there, then this question is legitimate, although the window of acceptability is dangerously brief. If you happen to fall into that narrow slot I will answer promptly:

"One is a boy, and one is a girl."

This answer is honest and accurate, but I'm absolutely setting you up. What transpires next is your personal watershed moment that harkens back to the great intelligence sorting experiment of 1897.

If you follow up with Question 3a, "Yeah, but are they identical?" then I'm afraid I can't help you. Depending on my mood, you'll get a gracious additional explanation of how that scenario is genetically impossible. If I'm less tolerant (so honestly, most days), I'm going to just stare at you really intently with a disappointed look on my face and then probably suggest you think about it really hard.

I'll elaborate here for someone's benefit. Imagine you're in an art class and you have to draw the anatomy of a nude man and later a nude woman. Don't make it creepy, just think technically. Do your two drawings look exactly the same? There's your answer. (The answer is no, they're not identical, because by definition and biology, boys' and girls' bodies are not identical.)

Question 4: "Are they natural?"

This question is both very presumptuous and completely inappropriate. Presumptuous because shame on you for thinking you deserve to know that. I always answer this question the same way:

"No, they're animatronic."

People don't usually like that answer. Good, because I don't like the question. Of course they're natural. They are humans. Natural? Really? I don't think that's a great term. Honestly, even the medical community seems to use this nomenclature. We were labeled with that handle in the NICU, where the nurses definitely all knew that our two were "natural" twins. It made the staff treat us differently. Better, I think, but that seemed unfair. I think the mentality was that some people with multiples "did this to themselves," whereas the natural twins' parents just got unlucky. First, I disagree, I feel lucky to have twins. Second, so what if there was some medical intervention? Does that make any of the babies any less important or less worthy of helping? Of course not. Let's stop with that natural label. I digress again.

Back to the question. After asking are they natural, some like to go further with the dangerous follow-up:

Question 4a: "You know, did you have any help?"

This is a deeply personal question and it's one hundred percent none of your business. I don't ask you about your personal life and private things going on with your body. Is that your real hair? Did you get liposuction? Are those her real…? You get the point. Those things are not my business, and my family fertility status is none of yours.

A Touchy Subject

Finally, my babies are not a tactile display at a museum sensory exhibit. I don't need or want you to touch my babies, or their stuff. If you're over for a visit and you ask, or I invite you to hold the baby, that's a totally different story, but you are not entitled to randomly reach into their spaces and touch their faces. When the twins were quite new and we finally ventured out to church with them, we kept blankets over their car seats. This was partially to keep out the cold winter air but was also deliberate to keep them protected from the germs of the public. Some older gal with good intentions came right up, tells me she's been sick, so she doesn't want to touch the babies, but wants to look at them. Before I can protest, she pulls down the blankets and rubs her hands all over the blankets covering their bodies. Umm, ick and no thanks. She meant well, but please, just don't. Yes, they are cute, but you're not entitled to that. Similarly, you shouldn't get right up in their face with your ugly mug. You wouldn't do that to me and my face, and I wouldn't do that to you, so don't do it to them. Also, let's admit it, your face is pretty scary up close and there's also the issue of your halitosis. See, you made me be mean again. Just back off a little please; stay behind the velvet ropes.

***

Ok, my back hurts from all the soapbox standing, but it needed to be said. Please, heed my warnings because I'm telling you, we all do and say these things. We don't mean to, but we do it. We can do better than this. You may now return to your regularly scheduled programming.

Part X - Living

The Nights are Long

We survived the NICU, survived the winter without the babies getting sick, and now we are starting to settle into new rhythms. Kylene is home with the kids during the day and keeps them entertained and on schedule and then I jump in as soon as I get home from work. Nights aren't easy, but our regimented schedule makes it mostly predictable. We have to supplement nursing with formula just to keep up with two babies, but since that means about half nursing and half bottles it allows me to take one of the two night feeding shifts. Early on, they needed to eat every two to three hours, but they're stretching more each week. Even now, with feedings every three to four hours, I can sometimes get anywhere from four to six hours of sleep since I only do one round of feedings. I've learned that I can survive the workday on four hours. It makes for a zombie-like existence, but I can do it, and I have done it many times.

I'm always aiming for a little more sleep and so to maximize my sleep quotient, my night feeding shift has become a game on several levels. Efficiency exemplified. First, it's always a matter of working around Roman. If he's awake, he gets fed first, plain and simple. Otherwise, he'll cry the entire time until it's his turn. Eden, on the other hand, will just lay there and wait. It's unfair, but he gets rewarded, and she gets penalized because his wailing wakes up Kylene and makes everyone miserable. So, the start of every feeding cycle is a check on what Roman is doing. If I arrive and he's sound asleep, I try to quietly feed Eden first before he wakes up. It's always a gamble, but I'm getting better at reading his restlessness and making my game time decision on who should go first.

Regardless, I've got the night feeding regiment down to a science. From the time my alarm goes off, I can do everything—get up, get the first bottle of formula, warm it up, feed, burp, and then change Eden, get the next bottle, warm it up, feed, burp, and change Roman, and be back in bed — in thirty minutes flat. Yes, I've timed it. There are other issues some nights, but on a good night, I lay back down after my shift feeling victorious, and Kylene never even stirs.

The feedings are the regular, planned visits to the nursery in the middle of the night, but there are many other visits for myriad reasons. Someone is always needing something. Lost pacifiers are usually the cause which finds me on my hands and knees, illuminated in the eerie green glow of LED nightlights searching for translucent green rubber pacifiers. Green and green. What horrible choices — the lighting makes it impossible as the colors are exactly the same. Since I can't see anything, I just feel around the crib or the floor, running my hands over the carpet until I find the jettisoned equipment and return it to the distraught mouth seeking its comfort. And if it's not searching for pacifiers, it's something else. There is always something. I get up a lot, and Kylene gets up more, but it's working as well as can be expected. Another of my mom's sage phrases echoes in my head again: *The nights are long, but the years are short.* She's right about the first part at least.

The nights pass, and then weeks and then months. We are surviving; I dare say we are even thriving. Yes, we are tired; my goodness we are *always* tired, but we are enjoying all of it.

Kylene is back to work part time and so we also mix daycare into our lives. We have begun a new routine of bottle and diaper prep every evening, drop offs in the mornings, pickups in the afternoons, and lots of look-ins on the webcam. Again, we adjust, and survive and even learn to thrive. We are crushing this parenting twins challenge.

The Trifecta

It's July and the twins are seven months. Summer has been hectic but memorable, filled with hauling large plastic exersaucers and pack-n-plays back and forth to the cottage every weekend. It's a lot of work but during naps we get to ski and do our fun things and we also have lots of family around who are keen to hold babies. Besides all that, this is my happy place, and I enjoy showing it to our kids and forging new memories here together.

We've just enjoyed a long weekend of fun and boating with our friends visiting from Chicago. They've departed, but we have stayed and are now looking forward to our annual week-long vacation here at the lake. It's a great time filled with family traditions that we share with several other families, and it's one that I look forward to every year.

Just as a wave of relaxation starts to envelop me, Kylene requests that I make a quick trip to the store to get a few things. I run to the store for diapers, formula, and baby food all the time but one of the items she wants this time is a pregnancy test. She assures me that can't possibly be pregnant, but she just wants to make sure.

My mind is racing, but I go, I return, she goes, we wait, and when the time is up, she makes me go look at the stick. On my way to the bathroom counter, she reiterates one last time how it's not possible. The stick says otherwise.

The exchange over the next few minutes is a little heated. Not angry, just surprised, confused, and did I mention surprised? The recipe of the conversation consists of some dashes of "how did this happen" sprinkled with "I am usually so regular," and a final garnish of her saying "I want you to be happy about this." I am, or I will be, I'm just scared right now.

We both spend the rest of the week in a fog as we get used to the idea of welcoming another blessing so soon. Then something else unexpected happens. One of our family friends invites her former college roommate to visit her at the lake at our cottage. Having extra visitors is common during this annual reunion week. There are plenty of chairs and we are all outside all day, so the more the merrier. Come and enjoy the lake. Unfortunately, when the friend arrives, it's pouring rain. An all-day soaker. Everyone, including dozens of people and five small kids, are all crammed in our small cottage living room. The friend's friend arrives anyway, with her three young kids in tow.

"How old are your boys?" someone asks as the guests settle in.

"These older two are twins, they're two, and my baby here is nine months."

"Wow, so how close in age are they?" someone else asks. She smiles and says, "They are fifteen months apart."

Amidst the murmurs of marvel at this spacing, I look across the room at Kylene and we share a knowing glance. The exact scenario we have coming is staring at us in the flesh. Twins and another one fifteen months behind.

Well, okay then, let's see what this dress rehearsal shows us.

I think we're both hoping for a heartwarming session of reassurance, but honestly, the next two hours are kind of a nightmare. The baby cries the whole time, and the twin boys are acting like boys, but are a bit out of control for my comfort level. I am admittedly hypersensitized to the whole situation, but oh my goodness, it is complete chaos. I was a little worried and a little scared before they arrived, but now I am terrified of what is coming for us.

All fears aside, I think it is important to reiterate right here, I am not unhappy about this news. I am thrilled. We love being parents, I love being a dad, and even though many people have remarked that we have the perfect little family, one boy and one girl, we have never thought we were done having kids. When the twins were born, there was no sense of completion. We have always wanted at least three, and now in the last few days it seems Kylene has emerged as the prognosticator that Grandma Smith once was. The three greasy pairs of hands eating grilled cheese sandwiches at the cottage bar stools, the impossible dream she was pining for, is coming true. As for me, I want this, but I'm struggling with how to best plan for it. It's the front car of the rollercoaster and we are climbing a record tall hill. I can be happy and scared at the same time.

Over the next week we get comfortable with this next chapter, the fear morphs into giddy joy, and we start getting really excited. Just like last time, we go through the strange ride of knowing a wonderful piece of information but choosing to wait to share it.

I am embracing the reality of our compressed family schedule, and I can't wait to meet the new little one, but right there is where my only fear remains. The little *one*. One. I'm still worried that it is two again. I love Roman and Eden, and I'm glad we had twins, but I'm scared of doing that again, especially since they'll be only fifteen months old when the baby comes. I don't dwell on this constantly, but the fear is always lingering and lurking in the background, leaning in through the window of my otherwise happy disposition. My apprehension culminates at the first ultrasound appointment, when the technician, per my request, looks around for multiples.

"Nope, I only see one in there."

Instead of relief, I respond with disbelief, doubting the thoroughness of her investigation, as if there are various uterine caverns still unexplored.

"Look again." I'm dead serious. "One could be hiding behind the one you're seeing. Let's double check."

She begrudgingly obliges and confirms it again. One baby. A girl. I've never been so relieved.

We can handle one. Piece of cake. And another girl? That's amazing.

My heart swells three sizes as my feelings for my newest baby girl solidify further. We're going to have three kids. All remarkably close together, they'll all grow up right in each other's business, all the time. It was all about the twins for a while, but that is going to change. There's another one coming to join the fun. The trifecta is on the horizon.

Shock and Awe

When the right time comes, we start telling everyone the news, and it's even more fun than the last time because everyone responds so intensely. It's hilarious to watch. Instead of overt happiness, everyone stares at us in disbelief, many ask new inappropriate questions or feel compelled to relay thoughts of concern that they suppose we haven't considered. Trust me, whatever you're thinking, we've thought of all that already. It is shocking, yes, but it is amazing. Such a blessing. We are so lucky.

Pregnancy proceeds smoothly, for me at least, with no real complications other than Kylene has regular heartburn. Crazy, constant heartburn. She carries Tums antacid tablets everywhere she goes. The old wives' tale suggests heartburn means the baby will be born with a lot of hair. We will see. Beyond that, the pregnancy, plus raising two babies, delivers various new levels of joy stirred with continuous exhaustion. We are happy, blessed, and loving life, even if it is being lived in a constant blur of fatigue, diapers, and a daily tornado of toys.

From about 29 weeks and forward I began mentally preparing for another early entrance. I preface every business meeting with warnings of "if the baby comes," but she never does. Baby girl is doing just fine. The due date is nearing but everything still looks good. Things have been going so well that I've started running and training for the Irish Jig, a local 5k race. I am ready to race, but I have postponed registration until the last minute just in case of baby action. Today is Friday and the race is tomorrow, so after work I finally go register, pay my fee, and get my race bib and t-shirt. The check-in reminds me of the positive racing atmosphere, and I arrive home excited for tomorrow, excited to race tomorrow. As I walk in the door at home, Kylene sees the bag of race swag in my hand and asks,

"Wait, did you register for the Jig?"

"Yeah, it's tomorrow morning."

"Oh. I'm pretty sure I'm in labor, I think I'm going to have the baby tonight."

"Umm. Okay. That would have been good information two hours ago, maybe even this morning?"

She tells me she didn't know then, but now she feels like she's been feeling something different all day. Contractions.

Again, couldn't this have been shared a little sooner?

She didn't know for sure then, but now it seems she does. It's happening.

Ok then, here we go. I shift into a different mode. Not panic per se, but his second cousin: anxious agitation. We need to get ready. Granted, the new nursery is ready, and our bags are packed, and we actually *are* fairly ready, but we need to get someone over here to watch the twins. My parents are already coming and Kylene's mom is on alert.

Ok, I guess we are ready then.

At least that's what I keep telling myself.

My parents arrive, eager to see the twins, and we grab our bags and head into the hospital. It's Friday night and we expect we'll meet our baby soon, maybe before midnight.

Late on Friday or maybe it's early Saturday by now, hours have passed, but we are still in labor and delivery triage land. The contractions keep coming and dilation is started, but progress has plateaued. The staff isn't in a hurry because Kylene isn't quite there yet. We're in labor limbo. Even so, because we know we are having another C-section, so we don't want to go too far and cause other trouble. Despite my urging and reminders, that factor isn't strong enough to push the medical team forward, so after many hours of monitoring and consistent contractions, but no more progress, we are dismissed and sent home with directions to come back when the contractions are less than five minutes apart.

Frustrated and a little disappointed, we return home, release my similarly disappointed parents, and settle in for a day of counting minutes. It's already Saturday now, and the race starts in like six hours. Of course I can't risk leaving, but I don't like leaving things undone or goals unaccomplished.

Oh well, at least I got my t-shirt.

We crash into bed, but after I've slept only a few winks, the twins stir awake, blissfully unaware of last night's excitement. Of course they don't know, but they are up, they need to eat, and they have a full itinerary of destroying the house planned for today. Since it is clear to all parties in the room that I am the one getting up, I saunter out of our room and stumble into theirs to begin the retrievals and start the day.

As tired as I am, there is no better greeting than the bright eyes of your child, waiting for you to come rescue them and pick them up. The smiles, the trust, the reunion after mere hours apart, and the outpouring of love. It's a gift and I get a double dose. There are two of them and I carry them both out at the same time. I'm a lucky man.

Rerun

Kylene's mom arrives a little later and once she's brought up to speed on the details, she isn't happy with the medical team instructions. She thinks we should go back right away. We aren't so keen on that idea, as we don't need another dismissal. The contractions continue and gradually get closer together, but they stall out at about five minutes apart and never become *less than* five minutes. Nuance perhaps, but Kylene is undeterred. We'll wait until the threshold is crossed. The twins are back to bed for the night, and I realize things are likely going to get interesting soon, so I tell Kylene I'm going to bed and to wake me up when she's close to ready. There's nothing I can do at this point, and she's the one deciding our next move anyway, so I retire.

I catch a few hours of much needed sleep until she gently wakes me up. She's not panicked or expressing urgency, just a clear message that we should probably get going. I'm groggy but unalarmed due to her calm. I get up and shower and prepare for the day even though it's near the middle of the night. We retrace our steps and end up at the same triage floor. This time, she is checked once, and a flurry of activity begins. Evidently, she's ready now; it just took twenty extra hours of discomfort. We are scheduled to go next, or close to next, and wouldn't you know it, Dr. Bateman is on call tonight. She's going to conduct the surgery.

This feels right.

A Time to Be Born

Kylene is taken back for prep, and I'm given scrubs and told to wait. I've done this all before, not that long ago really, but it is so much less tense than the last time that it doesn't feel the same. I'm ushered into the operating room and this part feels the same. How I feel, feels the same. I am a useless stump taking up space, positioned at the head of the bed, and expected to stay out of the way. I know better than to watch the incision this time and try to focus just on Kylene. Within a matter of minutes, Dr. Bateman extracts our baby girl and presents her to us. We cut the cord and I begin feeling a familiar sensation. My vision is tunneling, and I know that I need to sit down. The nurse asks,

"Would you like to hold your daughter?"

There is nothing I'd like to do more at this moment, but I force myself to reply honestly.

"Yes, I would really like to hold her, but I can't yet. I'm a little dizzy."

The brave knight needs his orange juice again. The moment has once again overwhelmed me. There is no stress of an emergency this time, no concerns over survival, it's just a big moment, and as full as my heart is, my head just needs a minute. I guess this is just what I do. This robot is programmed a certain way and needs to reboot.

The nurse returns, "Do you have a name?"

I toss a look at Kylene for confirmation and then reply, "Her name is Addison."

Then here come the stats, the ones I want and have been collecting.

APGARS 8 and 9

7 pounds 8 ounces

19 inches

Born at 2:52 am.

Addison. Addy. She weighs more than the twins combined, yet she's still so small and perfect, and a head full of dark black hair. That explains the heartburn. She has a look altogether different than either of the other two, but I am immediately in love.

I make the nurse write down all the numbers on a piece of paper, just like the other one in my wallet and that's when I notice the time of birth: 2:52 am. I guess it is Sunday after all, but more interesting is the time—2:52. The same time the twins were born. Theirs was 2:52 pm, but still, come on. What are the odds?

Ok, God, now you're just showing off.

Normal

When we leave the operating room, Kylene and Addy go to the same room for recovery. I guess this is the normal set-up for most new parents, but it's new to me. Having Addy in the same room with Kylene is momentous, a massive change from the last time we were here. Addy is right there in the clear plastic baby tub thing wrapped up in a blanket. She's three feet away. No equipment, no monitors, no wires, or hoses. I can pick her up any time I want. The whole situation is completely foreign.

Is this what it's normally like?

The nurse asks if she should take Addy to the nursery so Kylene can rest.

Umm no. The nurse doesn't know what we went through before. *No, I think our baby will stay right here, thank you.*

After Kylene gets settled, I head back home to sleep a few hours and to see the other two hooligans living under my roof. They still don't know what's going on, even though I tell them that mama's baby is coming home soon. Even so, it's good to see them briefly and connect before I head out again. I fill in Kylene's mom on the details and plan for her to come visit with the twins later in the day. I call my parents and my siblings and then head back to the hospital. Kylene is calmly holding Addy when I arrive. Quiet, serene, peaceful, and not at all stressful. It is still hard to grasp that this is how it's supposed to be.

Kylene and I talk about this very thing. We are both perplexed by the difference in experiences. Addy is just lying there, doing nothing. We are just sitting here, doing nothing. This version of birth is almost… boring. I'm good with boring, I'll take all sorts of boring if it means my baby is healthy and doesn't need extra care or a needle poked into her head, or a tube jammed down her throat. I'll take boring all day long.

Since we have nothing else to talk about, we begin to turn our focus outward and ask aloud whether anyone is going to come and visit.

Where is everyone?

With the sense of urgency and uncertainty removed from the situation, everyone, even the doting grandparents, are not disrupting their lives for an immediate trip. They are definitely coming, but they go to their respective churches, eat lunch, and then make their way to the city to see their new granddaughter. They all come, just not in terrified droves like last time. Normal seems to suit everyone a little bit better.

Party of Five

Kylene's mom eventually arrives with the twins, and they have miraculously gotten huge over the course of a few hours. They're still small, but juxtaposed relative to Addy, they are gigantic, and loud, and sweaty. We take our first family picture with all five of us and it is predictably horrible, but at the same time perfectly honest. We go zero for three on capturing the attention of the kids, and in every photo at least one is crying or whining, and no one appears all that happy or interested in the photo. The twins have no interest in Addy because there is just too much going on. The only attention Addy gets from them is Eden's irritation that she's in the way of hugging mama.

Another unexpected wrinkle emerges: apparently Roman is mad at Kylene. He won't let her hold him, he won't respond to her, and he only comes to me. Evidently, he's upset that she so selfishly left him to go give birth to his baby sister. How dare she? It is interesting and comical, but it makes Kylene a little sad. It's a new thing that I guess we'll have to deal with later.

Despite the relative chaos of the first encounter, being together as the Smith party of five feels good. It feels complete. I missed Roman and Eden, and I'm glad they're here. I'm also glad they are leaving soon since we don't have any toys or food in here for them and they'll be miserable. We'll all be leaving soon anyway and reconvening at home.

Another day goes by, Kylene is recovering well, and Addy is doing great. We're going to get released today. It feels so strange to leave with our baby so soon, after just a few days, but we are packed up and ready to wheel Kylene and Addy out to the car. Everyone is going home together. It is surreal, and I couldn't be happier.

We arrive home and put Addy in the pack-n-play with the bottom elevated like a high crib, set right in the living room. She can sleep in here while the other two do their normal toy tornado activities, at least for today. Both twins can crawl but, given they are a little behind from being preemies, they can't yet walk. Three non-walking, non-talkers in diapers at once. This will certainly be an interesting season of life.

Right after I set Addy down, Roman and Eden sense something new has entered their realm. They both crawl over, pull themselves up on the side of the pack-n-play and can just barely peek over the edge. They are investigating the new addition.

Their eyes and noises implore me with an unspoken question: "What is that thing?"

"That's the baby. That's Addy. She's home now."

We're all home. Together.

Part XI - Epilogue

The Real Heroes

You've undoubtedly surmised by now that even though I've set myself up as protagonist, narrator, and self-centered feature of the story, I'm not the hero. In fact, you may have already recast me as the villain or maybe the comic relief. The bumbling idiot who got a lot of things wrong, who failed at every turn, but maybe, just maybe, has some enduring, redeeming qualities because he meant well along the way.

The sequence of mishaps is one of many themes to this story, and one that continues as I raise my kids. Many times I considered starting a website or a blog or something chronicling my everyday parenting struggles. It would be called *Failing Daily*, or something like that, because I do fail on a daily basis. But that's what parenting is: trial and error. Error might mean failure, but error also means I learned something. Or at least I should have. Sometimes I fail the same way over and over. Regardless, I keep trying, because raising my kids is the single most important thing I'm doing. The most important thing I'll ever do. So, I keep trying and yes, I keep failing.

So back to the topic at hand, I'm not the hero here, but there are many who are featured and should be highlighted.

Our friend Tony helped me out, helped us out, and gave me a backstop of support on what turned out to be an important 24-hour segment of time. I'll always appreciate that. Now, I'm not sure if I mentioned it before, but I do sort of blame him for everything too. All of it. He brought Kylene a Wendy's Frosty, and it sure seems like that Frosty started the whole premature labor sequence. I can't prove it (not yet anyway), but I'm going to thank Tony and blame him at the same time nonetheless.

Kylene's sister Katie dropped everything to get Kylene to the hospital and stayed until I arrived. She would have stayed for days if she needed to. We needed her in a dire moment, and she came through with flying colors.

The rest of our families came too, and many of them came many times. We were in crisis, and they came to support us, with nothing to do but just be there. It meant the world to us, and we needed it. They helped a lot along the way too, from babysitting, to Kylene's sister Stefan rescuing us when we all got rotavirus, to my parents and Kylene's mom coming when Addy was born and the dozens of other things in between. We moved back home to Michigan for a reason, and this was it. Family is everything.

Doctor Bateman delivered all three of our kids, and she was always kind, attentive, and kept us (mostly) calm throughout what was some pretty scary stuff. I trusted her completely and that is not something I'm able to say very often about very many people. She means so much to me and to our family and we are forever grateful.

The NICU and NIM staff and the brain trust of doctors that looked after our twins. Much of what I say and write is heavy handedly laced with sarcasm, but this is not. I am sincerely thankful to them. I realize a lot of my collected anecdotes are about frustration and fear, a few less-than-perfect scenarios, and some staffers I asked to not come around anymore, but the majority of the care was excellent. Roman and Eden not only survived but thrived, because of that staff's expertise and devotion to our kids and to so many others just like ours. We wouldn't be where we are now without the efforts they all collectively gave, and I'll never, ever forget that. They saved my kids' lives and saved mine in the process.

I'm sure I'm missing some other contributors, so I'm sorry for that, but there are two more I need to address. Kylene is the real hero. She deals with me every day, and that alone is worth a series of increasingly expensive medals. She carried the twins, she had the surgery, she nursed them at the same time, she carried Addy while dealing with the twins, had another surgery, and then she dealt with the whole trifecta. I've been involved, maybe even more than most dads, but let's be real, Kylene has done—and continues to do—a tremendous amount of work. She's not perfect either, but she loves our kids, as much as I do. Without her, none of this happens. She is mom, their mom, the perfect one for them. She is the foundation of our family. She is a superhero.

Tears for Fears

(2020)

Many years after later, when Roman and Eden are around fourteen, and have completed their ten years at our local Christian school. As it is the tradition at our school, they each have to give a presentation about their journey, their growing faith, and what they've learned along the way. It's a big deal for the outgoing class and everyone knows about this annual project for the outgoing eighth graders. Parents are invited to attend the presentations, and when each student finishes speaking, there is time for parental commentary. Kylene usually defers to me in these types of situations, so I provide our response. As I congratulate Eden and express how proud we are of her, I get choked up and begin to cry. I didn't expect that to happen. Eden certainly didn't expect it, but it happens. An anomaly for sure. Roman's presentation is later the same day, and it happens again. I choke up, and there are tears. Fast forward to Addy's presentation a year later and once again, I'm crying.

It's a big event and a moving moment, so tears are perhaps understandable—for a normal person with a full range of normal, functioning emotions. But, as I've been told, and willingly admit, I'm not normal. This isn't the me I'm accustomed to. The last time I remember crying was at my Grandpa's Smith's funeral, when the twins were one. It's been thirteen years since then. Prior to that had been at my Grandpa Workman's funeral, eight years earlier. So twice in about twenty-one years. Mr. Roboto's programming doesn't allow for emotional displays. For better or for worse, I was locked down. Now I'm crying twice in one day? That's not me. Or at least I didn't think so.

Not long after the twins eighth grade presentations, the five of us find ourselves watching a movie at home about a guy, his dog, and eventually his family with that same dog. Even though we don't have any pets, the ending of the film starts to get rough for me. The dog is dying, and suddenly, I'm living a classic *Seinfeld* episode as I notice a "salty discharge" emerging from the corners of my eyes.

What in the world is this? I get up and leave the room, sort of to hide what has surprised even me. I'm crying again, and this time over a movie?!

What is happening? Umm. I was cutting onions. Leave me alone.

Time continues marching on, the kids are now all in high school, and it's happening more and more. Addy's first track race in high school, Division 1 track, against seniors. She flat out wins the race and I go misty-eyed. Roman makes a new PR in cross country or wins Outstanding Senior at the band awards night—I have sniffles. Eden wins the district championship and then the regional championship with her volleyball team. Salty leaks again. And of course, when Eden hands off to Addy in the state finals of the 4x400 track relay, my heart is in my throat.

You might conclude that I've simply gone soft in my old age. That might be right, but I think there's more to it than that.

I've tried so hard, so intentionally, to have an impact on these kids, but the tables have turned; frankly, they turned a long time ago. *They* are the ones having an impact on *me*. My kids have captured my heart and upgraded my life in so many amazing ways, and they haven't just changed my life; they've changed me.

I'm still flawed, but I'm (slightly) less impatient, less rigid, more caring, and more thoughtful. We still have our moments of conflict like any family, but as my mom pointed out all those years ago, I just love so deeply. She was right.

I love these kids so much and I'm so invested in them and everything that they do that it moves me at unexpected times and in unexpected ways. They have penetrated my armor, stripped it away and left me raw and vulnerable, and now, evidently that means crying. They have engineered me into a better person, broken down all the barriers, and forced me to let all the feelings out, whether in private or in public. Or even in a book. They have deprogrammed the robot.

The Clearest Lens

If you're paying close attention, you may have noticed that in the heroes chapter I mentioned there were two more heroes, and then I only explained one. You're right; good catch, that's what this chapter is for.

You've probably gathered by now that I am a Christian man. That statement doesn't make me anything special and I'm certainly not better than anyone else. Far from it. I am horribly flawed, and I mess things up all the time and am probably a terrible hypocrite in many ways. You might even have a list of my flaws running in your head or in the margin of the book (or in a conditionally formatted spreadsheet). I accept that, and I'm working on it, but let me warn you—I'm going to mess up again. Even though I am an engineer, that is my nature, as a human. We are all broken, and we all need redemption that is not of our own accord. I believe that.

Another part of my faith is that I believe there is more to life than just what we're doing here on Earth and what we have planned, and

I believe it is all connected and important. Eternally important. I believe God has larger plans and purposes.

I don't think that means we should just sit around and do nothing. We should be active, intentional participants in life. God gave us minds, bodies, and motivations. We are supposed to do things, work hard, and try our best—even if we fail. We are even supposed to plan and achieve, but we need to understand God's plan is bigger, and ultimately, he is in control.

I'll admit, I didn't always see that. I grew up going to church, Sunday school, and catechism class. I went to Christian school, I met and married a Christian girl, and our kids do all the same things that we did: school, church, the whole works. I was raised in a culture of faith, and I'm thankful for that head start, but that faith didn't become mine until I got older, specifically through personal epiphanies in high school and college. Up until then, and even after, my pursuit of control and self-made armor shielded me from being open to how God could work in my life.

Even with some revelations and acceptance of things in my own heart, I was usually hampered by being so, well, being so *me* about everything. My teens and twenties were marked by a drive to be perfect so that I could achieve everything through my own efforts and to succeed because of my planning. With my sense of all-encompassing control, I thought I was making all the things happen while God was relegated to a prayer ATM that I turned to every once in a while when things went awry. I didn't ever lose my faith or conduct myself in shockingly unsavory ways, I just didn't live with and by faith very convincingly. I didn't rely enough on God.

I failed to see my life through the lens of what God had planned for me. I was too stubborn, or too stupid, or I just never had the vision to grasp it in the moment. Honestly, I probably just didn't look very hard. I was focused on what I was doing, but now, I am beginning to see things much more clearly.

I guess hindsight is usually pretty clear, but even when you're looking back, it's easy to dismiss things as coincidence and slide right past obvious signs, or chalk them up to individual choice, or chance or fate or something else. You may think many of those things, but I believe otherwise.

I believe I suffered through a few things in middle school and those breakups in high school so that when I met Kylene, I wouldn't mess it up early and so that our friendship could grow before we dated. God knew that I was supposed to be with Kylene, but he also knew I was wounded, hard-headed, and hard-hearted when we met.

I believe we couldn't find good housing options in Chicago for a reason, so we would turn our hearts toward home and move back to Michigan. I believe this happened specifically so that when the twins came early just over a year later, we would be fifteen minutes from one of the best neonatal facilities in the state, not to mention surrounded by family. I can't even imagine how our experience would have played out differently had we still been in Chicago. I'm convinced it would have been so much worse, more logistically complicated, and infinitely more painful because we would have been alone. God knew that we needed that NICU and that we needed family around us.

I believe I took that job in Grand Rapids, one that I left after only ten months, so that I could get us home, and so that I would meet Adam, and Stephanie, two people I still consider close friends. Stephanie is married to Tony, the Frosty bringer, and Adam is married to Kim, who connected us to Anne. God knew we needed to know Anne, that she might have helped save our kids' lives in the NICU, and that she would teach us how to keep them safe when we went home. God also knew Kylene needed that Frosty.

I believe our unexpected NICU friends Jamie and Kendra came into our lives at the perfect time, bringing with them a flood of positivity, shared experience, and pure friendship. The relationship started because of their efforts and their smiles, and they persisted in connecting with us despite our insular behaviors at the time. We needed that joy, camaraderie, and perspective that only they could provide. After we left the hospital, Kendra and Kylene remained close, and they could always talk and relate to each other about the privileges and perils of multiples. Though we don't see them as much these days, we still stay connected, and they are still very special to us. God knew we needed Kendra and Jamie.

I believe that my first Grand Rapids job got us home, but that I was led to change to the next one specifically for the insurance. My company's insurance was incredible. We piled up three weeks in the NICU and the NIM for two babies, plus a C-section surgery. I opened the bills and gulped as I read the numbers. The total was well over $100,000. We could have been crushed financially for years by that sum, even with just a fraction of that invoice, but in the end, I paid $600 total. When I realized that, it made me laugh out loud. God knew I needed that job, that experience, and that we needed that insurance.

I believe Kylene left her auditing job and got the new one in Rockford the spring before the pregnancy began specifically for the flexibility her new job would eventually provide. She went on bed rest, and then we had the babies early, and then they extended her leave to begin when the twins were supposed to be born, not when they were actually born. Then, they let her come back part time, all the while holding her position for her. That company was extremely generous and accommodating to us. God knew we needed that flexibility.

I believe I was shaped and molded into the flawed robotic human that I am. God engineered me to be a husband to my wife and a dad to these kids. I still fail daily, but I was precisely made for this role. I believe these kids came at just the right time, all of them, and are perfectly made to bring me joy and challenge, to make me better and to fulfill my life, and to make this world better for the many who know and love them. God knew we needed these kids, these exact ones, at those exact times, and that His world needed these people in it.

You may scoff and say these are all coincidences, that things just happen, but I don't believe that. Not one bit. I see it all so vividly now as I look back at it all through a new lens — the clearest lens I've ever had.

Eighteen Years Later

(2023)

I open my wallet today and still have the piece of paper from the day I became a father. The APGAR scores. To me, those weights and those scores on that little paper represented the beginning of these premature gifts, these new lives, and a new beginning of me as I stepped into the role I was always meant for: being a father. I have Addy's APGAR scores paper too, memorializing the moment she completed our family. It's just paper, but I can't bring myself to part with the notes. The papers have become totems, reminders of their first moments, and a way for me to always be connected to them.

Roman and Eden turn eighteen later this month and it feels like this era is starting to wane. It has gone so fast. Too fast. They both started out behind, and small. They crawled late, they walked really late, and the doctors were generally spot on when they said it would take two years to catch back up. It took some time, but they caught up and ultimately flourished. They've done so well, and I'm so proud of them — of all three of them — and there is so much more to share but let me close the loop on some of the things I've left unanswered, and then brag gratuitously for a few pages.

Eden's hearing: she can hear fine, except as teenagers, none of them seem to hear anything, but that has nothing to do with her auditory capabilities. We never had another hearing issue after that first failed test. Much ado about nothing.

The issue with Eden's foot, it turned out, was exactly what our pediatrician said it would be. The angle of her foot was positional from the tight confinement in utero and within a few weeks of being out, it spun right back to normal on its own. Her foot is fine, and if anything, she is exceptionally gifted in her feet and legs.

Eden is tall, five feet nine inches, and is an incredible athlete; she always has been. She's a middle hitter on her varsity volleyball team and she can fly. There are other girls who are taller, but nobody jumps like her. I love watching her play and especially watching her elevate, float for a moment, and then crush the ball down in someone else's face. Over the years she played lots of soccer too and scored lots of goals with that supposedly damaged foot. She played lots of basketball and still plays on her varsity team. Eden is also an exceptional track athlete and has run in several events at the state championship, including the 400, and the 4x400 relay in which she hands off to Addy. You can't even imagine how that event and the Smith-to-Smith handoff makes my heart soar (and sometimes my eyes water). Anyway, Eden is amazing, and her foot is fine.

Eden was always tall, and Roman was always on the taller side of his class too, but he was shorter than Eden until about seventh grade. It was a point of contention for him, to be shorter than his twin sister. Then one day he passed her by and never looked back. He's now over six feet tall. He looks me right in the eye and desperately would like to pass me too. I think he will, either by a little more extension on his end, or my eventual withering decay as I age.

Roman, much like his father, was a solidly mediocre athlete in the middle years, but unlike his father has become an absolute powerhouse runner in both cross country and track. His progression throughout high school is nothing short of amazing and he has worked his way to becoming an all-conference and all-region runner, while serving as captain of his state-ranked high school cross country team. College running programs are starting to notice. You'd never believe he was three pounds at birth. Wimpy white boy indeed. No word on whether his alpaca impersonation skills are still present, but he is a naturally funny guy with a quick mind, sharp wit, and a great sense of humor. He has always liked to laugh and he's good at making me laugh. He is an incredible person.

Cognitively, I don't know if there was ever any concern from their preemie beginnings, but they were always fine. A preschool Sunday school teacher at church once told me they were both "wicked smart," and he was right. They excelled in school from the very beginning, from early elite math and spelling groups, to being co-valedictorians in eighth grade, and then on to achieving incredible heights in high school. As college applications have been submitted and we wait for results, I know they will have many amazing options. Of course, I still worry about things and try to control outcomes, but I'm completely confident in them. They will do well in whatever they choose to pursue.

Even though she didn't start in the NICU, I can't leave out Addy, because she is just as important as the twinkies. She completed our family. She was born into a scenario with two other kids about her age and I don't think her young mind ever considered that she might be smaller or less ready for anything than they were.

She taught herself to read at four, she learned to ride her bike the same day as the twins, and she has never felt behind in anything. They all did the same things and did them well, and Addy was always right there with them. Her athletic and academic achievements are just as rich, she was also valedictorian of her eighth-grade class, she is also a state qualifying runner in both cross country and track, and much like the other two, I have every confidence that she will find great success in life.

I don't consider this an ending, because there is more of the twins' senior year left, and another year with Addy home, and because I will keep parenting until the day I die, maybe even beyond if some of the wisdom I've passed on endures. Maybe it's just the midlife crisis talking, but even though this isn't the absolute ending of anything, it is the end of an era.

I watched them learn to walk and heard the funny things they said. I taught them how to ride a bike, how to ski, and how to waterski. I coached them in basketball, soccer, and all the things in between. We built Legos and obstacle courses, went on hikes, and collected leaves.

We ran in the sprinklers and played in the snow. I sang them silly songs, saw them sing in little plays, then I watched them star as the leads in school plays. I listened to concerts, attended awards ceremonies, and was present when they made their professions of faith. I spent hundreds of hours on sidelines, in bleachers and everywhere else imaginable, cheering my head off as they competed. I talked them through tears and nursed them through sickness and injuries. I was there for all of it. The messy and the perfect, the tough and the good.

We took them to cities and national parks and on vacations. I remember going to Disney when they were little, and everything still seemed real to them. We took them to New York City, and they wanted to sleep with the window open to hear the traffic. We explored the Badlands and Yellowstone, and the Tetons. We hiked Angels Landing, the Grand Canyon, and the Superstition Mountains. I remember white water rafting in West Virginia with Eden sitting with perfect posture in the raft, smiling the whole way, unafraid. I remember running in the mountains of Colorado with Roman, both of us huffing and puffing and learning together how hard high-altitude exertion can be. I remember swimming in the frigid waters of Jackson Lake with Addy, shivering and then dunking ourselves, simply because we were there.

I could go on like this forever as there are endless moments to recall. Some were extraordinary, some ordinary, and some mundane. Some brought boredom, some brought exhilaration, some brought arguments, and some brought laughter. I'm thankful for all of them because all the moments happened to us. Together.

If I graph out my life with all the variables considered, the results are clear: I am at about midlife. As I continue to process that, I'm realizing I've seen and done many things, and accomplished a great deal. More importantly though, I recognize that I *am* many things to many people: a son, a brother, a husband, a friend, and, yes, I'm still an engineer. Embodying each of these roles is a gift. I'm also a dad and being a father is the greatest gift. I've been blessed to be a dad for eighteen years already, I'm grateful for every second of it, and I'm ready for eighty more. My kids are by far my greatest accomplishment and make my life richer every day. I couldn't have engineered it any better.

Acknowledgements

This first book has been an incredible undertaking, harder than I expected, but also more enjoyable than I ever dreamt. I learned a lot in the process both about writing and about myself. I also realized I couldn't complete this project without help, and there are so many people I want to thank.

Thank you to my friend Chris, whom I've known since 2011. In our many hours together, you have become a trusted advisor, former (and future) running partner, a patient guitar teacher, and so many other things. You see my worst but always pull out my best. You've made me a better person in nearly every way. You, more than anyone, encouraged me to dive in and write this book, and then you were my cheering section along every step of the journey, not to mention my graphic designer. I simply couldn't have done this without you.

Thank you to my friend and coworker Laurel whom I've worked with for over twelve years. As a lead in our corporate Knowledge Sharing group, you are a gifted communicator, and have an amazing way of taking my often excited, but disjointed ideas, and massaging them into realistic deliverables. I have always enjoyed working with you whenever I can. That connection led me to set up the meeting when I randomly asked you to help me personally by editing my memoir. Given you're a young, working mother with plenty to do, it was an unfair request. You accepted anyway. Thank you for being my most thorough and scathing editor. Your honesty and perspective exposed some of my writing flaws yet affirmed me in the most vulnerable chapters. You made the story and my storytelling better.

A huge thank you to Nelson, my friend from church, who is an award-winning law professor, gifted (retired) attorney, and one of the most efficient people I know. He also happens to have authored over sixty books. Nelson, you encouraged me to write the book and gave me reams of excellent advice on how to start, how to finish, and how to publish. You also served as the world's fastest editor — sending it back to me, twice, with tons of edits, in less than twenty-four hours. I still don't know how you did that, but I'm thankful you did.

To our NICU friends Kendra and Jamie, who are featured stars in the book, thank you for reading this and for letting me share just a small slice of your incredible story. I can't believe our twinkies are done with high school. Keep doing what you do best — being amazing parents and people.

Thank you to my cousin Tamara who I asked to be a reviewer due to her twenty-five years of experience as a NICU nurse. Thank you for correcting my mistakes and misunderstandings, and clarifying how some things today are different compared to our NICU journey in 2005. Your input was critical, and hopefully I got it mostly right.

Finally, to my family, thank you for letting me write this and put it out in public. To my wife Kylene, though the words and thoughts are mine, the journey was ours, and we were always in it together, even when we were logistically apart. To my kids, Eden, Roman, and Addy, though you might not be thrilled about this story now, I hope someday you'll choose to read and appreciate it, because regardless of whether anyone else reads this book, it was always meant for you.

About the Author

Ross J. Smith holds bachelor's and master's degrees in structural engineering from the University of Michigan and is a licensed professional engineer in three states. Working over twenty years in forensic engineering has provided an endless succession of challenges, opportunities, and intrigue as he investigates damages from fires, floods, tornados, and structural collapses. While he has an exciting career, Ross' greatest love and adventure is his family. After a decade away, Ross and his wife returned to their hometown of Grand Haven where they raised their three children near the sandy shores of Lake Michigan. When he's not cheering his kids at sporting events or recording their band and orchestra concerts, you can find Ross chasing flat water on his slalom ski, seeking powder, moguls, and glades in the mountains, running along the lake, or leading worship at his local church.

www.ingramcontent.com/pod-product-compliance
Lightning Source LLC
Chambersburg PA
CBHW070748160726
48004CB00001B/105